CA Proficiency 2
Strategic Finance and Management Accounting Toolkit

CA Proficiency 2
Strategic Finance and Management Accounting Toolkit

Published in 2008 by
Institute of Chartered Accountants in Ireland
Burlington House, Burlington Road
Dublin 4

ISBN: 9780903854504

Copyright of publication rests in entirety with the Institute of Chartered Accountants in Ireland (ICAI). All rights reserved. No part of this text may be reproduced or transmitted in any form or by any means, including photocopying, Internet or e-mail dissemination, without the written permission of the ICAI. Such written permission must also be obtained before any part of this document is stored in a retrieval system of any nature.

The opinions expressed in this publication are those of the author and do not necessarily represent the views of the ICAI. The text is designed to provide accurate and authoritative information in regard to the subject matter covered. It is sold on the understanding that the ICAI is not engaged in rendering professional services. If professional advice or other expert assistance is required, the services of a competent professional should be sought.

© *CA Proficiency 2 Strategic Finance and Management Accounting Toolkit,* Institute of Chartered Accountants in Ireland, 2008

CONTENTS

	BACKGROUND	1
SESSION 1	FINANCIAL STRATEGY: FORMULATION AND ENVIRONMENT	3
SESSION 2	INVESTMENT DECISIONS, FINANCING DECISIONS AND DISTRIBUTION DECISIONS	25
SESSION 3	RISK DECISIONS	45
	SOLUTIONS TO TASKS 1 TO 35	57
SESSION 4	PERFORMANCE MEASUREMENT	117
	SOLUTIONS TO TASKS 36 TO 57	142

PATHWAY TO COMPETENCY IN STRATEGIC FINANCE AND MANAGEMENT ACCOUNTING

BACKGROUND

You are James Crown and you have just completed your undergraduate degree and have been awarded your degree and achieved a 2.1. This means that you have been offered a training contract with Sonner & Saville, a Chartered Accountancy training firm. You have always wanted to be a CA and have always had your eye on getting a training contract with Sonner & Saville as it has the reputation of being a firm that will afford you a wide breadth of experience throughout the period of your training.

Jeanne Sonner is the managing partner, having taken over from her father who has now retired. There are four other partners in the firm. They are:

Kim Lu	Harry O'Neill	John Keane	Brenda Perry
Taxation	Corporate Finance	Audit	Professional Standards
Partner	Partner	Partner	Partner

Your training will provide you with experience in all of these areas.

When you arrived in Sonner & Saville you were pleased to see that Catherine Clarke, whom you knew vaguely from your student days, is also a trainee CA with the firm. As you both have completed relevant business degrees, the partners assume that you have a sound theoretical knowledge across the various disciplines.

In your first week in the office the partners just want you to familiarise yourself with the Sonner & Saville way of doing business. They also take you to lunch, and because you already know Catherine they invite her along as well. During lunch, Harry O'Neill, the Corporate Finance Partner spoke on the merits of becoming a CA, and he emphasised at great length to you the relationship between your training and education. He knew that you would not be terribly busy this week and suggested that you might, in the first instance, read the Financial Strategy statement published by the Institute, and he reminded you that you will need a strong theoretical understanding of the various areas to carry out your work in this area satisfactorily during the period of your training contract. Have a read of the statement now www.icai.ie

SESSION ONE
FINANCIAL STRATEGY FORMULATION AND ENVIRONMENT

FINANCIAL STRATEGY FORMULATION AND ENVIRONMENT

> At the end of this session you should be competent in:
> - Understanding of the role of the CA in the framing of financial strategy and objectives including:
>   - Assessing a business's current position
>   - Explaining different stakeholders' perspectives.
> - Identifying government and professional regulations in financial management

You have completed your first six months in the practice of Saville, Sonner and Co, Chartered Accountants and you are now being assigned to the Corporate Finance Department within the firm for a period of your training. You go towards Harry O'Neill's office and his PA introduces herself and says: "Harry is out of the office today. As part of your preparation for working in this department Harry wants you to understand the finance function and the role of financial strategy in particular, and he has left you a document to read. This document, Appendix 1, is at the end of this section and you should then to summarise it's content for yourself and give a copy of your summary to Harry". You should also study carefully *Chapter 2* of the text, *Finance: Theory and Practice (Ward)* and complete the worked examples in order to understand the department's role.

6   STRATEGIC FINANCE AND MANAGEMENT ACCOUNTING TOOLKIT

> **Task 1: You are required to produce a one/two page summary explaining the purpose of financial strategy and its link to business strategy. Your note should identify the key stakeholders in the business and their different financial perspectives.**

Assessing the financial position of a business

Assessing where we are financially is a key skill needed before we get involved in the detailed financial planning. As a starting point you need to understand where the business is going if you are to be able to ensure that the appropriate finance is in place as well as to manage the investments in fixed assets and working capital to ensure that the shareholder objectives are met.

Harry O'Neill commends you on the content of your summary note and indicates that he expects that from your studies you are familiar with the topic financial analysis. He suggests that you should read *Chapter 3* of your text, *Finance: Theory and Practice,* (Ward), Financial Statement Analysis, to re-familiarise yourself with the topic and to complete the worked examples contained in the chapter.

A client of your firm whom Harry takes care of is Wonder Bathrooms Ltd. It has the following capital structure:

	£/€'000
Ordinary shares (5m shares of £/€ 1 each)	5,000
6% Preference shares	2,000
	7,000

Profits before tax in 20X8 were €/£ 1.5m and tax is payable at 20%.

> **Task 2: Harry asks you to calculate the Earnings Per Share (EPS) for 2008.**

How might financial targets be used and how might these trends impact on the future financial plans?

Having completed Task 2, Harry indicates that he wishes you to prepare a fininacial projection for a client, Food Co. You have noted that the company has a number of financial targets which it will use to plan and assess performance.

From the briefing documentation you identify the following:

Food Co is introducing a formal scheme of long range planning. Sales of their organic yoghurts have expanded rapidly over recent years due to increased health consciousness amongst their customers and significant growth is anticipated. In the current year sales are estimated at €4m and this is expected to grow to €4.3m, €5.2m, €7.4m, €8.2m and €9m over the next five years. The anticipated net profit after tax is anticipated to be 10% of sales and this is expected to remain constant over the planning period. Total assets less current liabilities are expected to remain at approximately 130% of sales. The finance director has suggested the following targets:

- Dividends should rise in line with the growth in profits;
- Retention of earnings should be 50% of profits and should remain unchanged;
- The rate of long term borrowing to long term funds (debt + equity) should be restricted to 35% (as happens to be the current gearing level).

	Current year	Year 1	Year 2	Year 3	Year 4	Year 5
	€m	€m	€m	€m	€m	€m
Sales	4.00	4.30	5.20	7.40	8.20	9.00
Net profit after tax						
Dividends						
Total assets less current liabilities						
Equity (increases by retained earnings)						
Maximum debt						
Funds available						
(Shortfalls) in funds						

8 STRATEGIC FINANCE AND MANAGEMENT ACCOUNTING TOOLKIT

> **Task 3: You are required to prepare a financial analysis of the draft long term plan.**

From your previous studies you will be aware that the provision of financial services operates within a specific legal framework. Harry calls you into his office and indicates that you will be accompanying him to a meeting with a potential new client later that day. In preparation for the meeting Harry refers you to an update on the legal framework contained in **Appendix 2** at the end of this section. He asks that you read this in preparation for the meeting.

You join Harry in the meeting room with the potential new client later in the afternoon. Mr Sahib introduces himself as a businessman and he indicates that he has come to Ireland to set up in business and hopes to invest in property and other activities over the next few years. He indicated that he had significant business interests overseas. During the meeting he reaches over to his brief case and on opening it you note that it appears to contain a large amount of cash. He indicates that he would wish your firm to open a bank account on his behalf. Given that he has no local utility bills he suggests that funds should be lodged in the firm's own bank account. He proceeds to mention that he hopes that his children can come to Ireland to be educated in the near future.

> **Task 4: Following the meeting you are required to draft a short email to Harry identifying any specific concerns that you may have.**

Appendix 1

What is the purpose of financial management?

Financial management can be defined as the management of the company's finances in order to achieve the financial objectives of the organisation. For private sector organisations this is normally taken to be to maximise shareholder wealth.

What are the elements of financial management?

Financial management is often presented as involving three decisions

- the **financing decision** (what funds do we need? What will be our sources of funds?);
- the **investment decision** (which capital expenditure projects should be undertaken? How can working capital management be improved?); and
- ultimately the **distribution decision** (having hopefully managed the business to ensure that we are profitable what proportion of our profits should be paid out). By retaining funds in the business we are increasing our equity base. All of these three decisions will be guided by the objective of maximising shareholder wealth.

As a starting point the chartered accountant will need to understand the business strategy so that the appropriate business planning can be developed and implemented. This is why we started with the notes outlining the stages of business strategy.

What is involved in financial planning?

The chartered accountant as financial controller or finance director will need to plan so as to ensure that there is sufficient funding available to meet the needs of the business over the short, medium and long- term. Typically the cash position will be monitored daily or weekly. On a monthly or quarterly basis cash budgets will be prepared and actual cash flows will be monitored against the plan to highlight short falls or surpluses so actions can be taken as needed. Over a longer term cash flow statements can be used to identify the longer term needs.

The focus in the short term is on cash and working capital management. We will be seeking to maintain liquidity (funds) to meet our immediate needs, for example. In the short term funds will be needed to purchase stock, cash will need to be collected from debtors and this is a time consuming activity for the accounts staff.

In the medium term funding will be needed for such items as the purchase of fixed assets. The financial planning for investments and acquisitions will identify additional financial needs which will need to be met. Arranging funding needs to be done in sufficient time, using appropriate sources (leasing, bank finance or equity) and remembering the need to match the life of the investment with the term of the finance.

What about financial control?

It should be clear that much of the time the chartered accountant is spent on monitoring the performance of the organisation against the agreed plans. Typical questions would include: Are the various parts of the business meeting their financial objectives? Are assets being used efficiently? (Ratios can come in useful here). Typically performance will be monitored against the planned or forecasted performance. Ideally, significant variances in performance will be highlighted quickly so that corrective action can be taken in a timely way.

What is the link between financial objectives and business (or corporate) strategy?

Strategy can be defined as a course of action including the specification of resources required to achieve a specific objective. In simple terms it is where we want to get to and how we wish to get there!

Any strategy can be short-term, medium- term or long-term depending on the time horizon it is intended to achieve. The definition makes clear that the starting point in strategy is to know and agree our objectives. Once we have determined our business strategy, this in turn will drive our financial strategy.

What is the purpose of strategic financial management?

Strategic financial management is the identification of the possible strategies capable of maximising an organisations net present value, the allocation of scarce resources amongst competing opportunities and the implementation and monitoring of the chosen strategy in order to ensure the achievement of the agreed objectives.

Our strategies will be **driven by the corporate strategy**. In this way the financial strategy can be seen as *supporting and aligned* to the business strategy rather than the driver per se. You will recall from your earlier studies that maximisation of net present value should ensure the maximisation of shareholder wealth. Additionally the definition highlights the need to allocate scarce resources and the ongoing requirement to monitor our progress.

What are typical corporate objectives and how do these relate to financial objectives?

In the section dealing with business strategy there was a discussion of corporate strategy and this highlighted the role of corporate objectives. Corporate objectives are relevant to the organisation as a whole. Ideally such objectives should be SMART – Specific, Measurable, Achievable, Realistic and Time-bound. Corporate objectives should be structured around the key aspects which determine business success. These might typically cover such things as:

- Desired level of profitability or return;
- Desired level of market share;
- Target growth rate;
- Customer satisfaction;
- Employee satisfaction or perhaps turnover;
- Quality standing of the firm's products.

It is worth stressing that the end of the business is not just profit per se. Having good standing with our customers and quality products are as likely to contribute to the long term profitability!

Financial objectives will be linked to the overall purpose of the organisation, which for business would normally be expressed to maximise shareholder wealth or at least provide an appropriate level of return for a given level of risk (what is termed the opportunity cost of capital). Typical financial objectives will thus be set for such things as:

- Target earnings, or earnings per share;
- Dividend per share;
- Desired level of retentions: a target level of dividend cover might be set;
- Target level of profitability: as measured by a target return on capital employed or net margin (profit/sales %);
- Target level of gearing: a target level of gearing might be set.

The board and senior management should periodically monitor actual performance against these targets over the longer term. As short term measures it is possible to manipulate results (perhaps by deferring capital expenditure or cutting back on training or R&D), though such actions are likely to be detrimental in the longer term. Having a number of objectives will lead to some conflict and in order to resolve this conflict, it is helpful to think of objectives as being primary (linked to profit) and secondary. Any conflict or inconsistencies should be discussed and appropriate compromises should be determined at a senior level.

How do we maximise shareholder wealth?

In a later section of the course you will examine share valuation. For the moment we can consider three broad ways in which shares might be valued:

- Balance sheet value: The assumption here is that the business is a going concern. As the values of some of the assets are based on historic values, such a valuation is unlikely to be adequate.
- Break-up basis: Here the assumption is that the company is to be wound up and its assets sold for other use – such a valuation would be appropriate for an "asset stripper".
- Market values: This is most likely to be the most sensible valuation though for a listed company a takeover can involve a significant unquantified premium. The current share price for a listed company would be the starting point. For a private company any valuation will involve a level of subjectivity.

The wealth of shareholders comes from the dividends received and the valuation of the shares. Shareholders will typically wish to see a rising share price over time. A successfully managed business should be able to produce a steady stream of rising profits, some of which are likely to be retained and reinvested. Good prospects are likely to have a positive impact on the share price and make it easier for the company to raise additional finance to support the business expansion. The opposite is also true. Additionally in the short term market sentiment can leave certain companies and sectors as unattractive to many shareholders and result in a depressed share price.

The company's management do not directly control the share price – indeed to seek to manipulate the share price in any way is illegal. Management should set itself appropriate financial targets which, if met should ensure a favourable market view of the company and thus a rising share price.

The theory of maximisation of shareholder wealth is based on economic theory. Economic profit is closer to cash than the typical accounting definition. You should appreciate from your studies that accounting profits can be manipulated at least in the short term perhaps through our choice of accounting policies. Examples might include the decision to capitalise some expenses, adding additional overheads into stock values or accelerating depreciation charges. In the end of the day profits are short term measures and a true measure of performance is likely to arise over a longer term.

What other non-financial objectives might be set for an organisation?

Most organisations are likely to have a number of additional objectives which will act as constraints on our goal of maximising shareholder wealth – at least in the short term. For example:

- To act responsibly towards the environment: In acting in a "green" way we are recognising our broader responsibility to the wider society and perhaps we could (like the Body Shop) use this as a way of differentiating ourselves.
- To support the welfare of employees: Addressing the welfare of employees is likely to result in lower staff turnover and increased staff morale and loyalty. Where staff have to be let go there is merit in paying above the minimum requirements of the law in terms of the potential benefits to remaining staff morale.
- To act responsibly towards our suppliers: Paying our suppliers on time for example in line with agreed terms of trade and avoiding using a dominant position in the market. In dealing fairly with our suppliers we are seeking to enhance our reputation and to build sustainable relationships.
- To satisfy the needs of our customers: This covers such things as acting fairly and ethically with our customers, providing appropriate customer support and so on. In so doing we are trying to build customer loyalty.

There are many more potential non-financial objectives, what is important is to recognise how these can constrain profitability in the short term but which could perhaps enhance the business in the longer term.

Who are the key stakeholders in an organisation?

So far we have argued that the organisation should seek to maximise shareholder wealth. Of course the shareholders are only one of the organisation's stakeholders. Indeed the non-financial objectives listed above seek to recognise the existence of other stakeholders. Stakeholders are individuals or groups who are affected by the activities of our organisation. They are often classified as internal (those who work for the organisation such as management and staff), connected (shareholders, customers and suppliers) and external (local community or government).

You will easily appreciate that each of the stakeholders will have different and often conflicting objectives and expectations in terms of the organisation. For example:

- As an employee your concern will focus on such things as terms of employment, security of employment;
- As a shareholder the concern is with maximising one's wealth subject to an acceptable level of risk;
- As a lender one will wish to see that the loan is repaid when due with appropriate interest and that loan covenants are honoured and any security is not prejudiced;
- As manager one will wish to maximise one's salary and rewards;
- The government will wish to see employment opportunities and compliance with laws;
- The local community will wish to see employment and probably some engagement with the community for example sponsorship of events.

The differing expectations of the stakeholders and their influence will impact on the strategy of the organisation. Typically some stakeholders will have more power and influence and their views will tend to prevail but the power can vary over time. The privatisation of organisations will result in greater power being in the hands of the shareholders for example.

How can the conflict of the different stakeholder perspectives be resolved?

If we take the example of managers and shareholders. Legally managers are agents of the shareholders and are assumed to act in the best interest of the shareholders. Management self-interest may however inhibit managers acting in this way. For example managers could pay themselves high salaries and perquisites and be inefficient. In private companies the shareholders and the managers may be the same people and thus the conflict should not arise. In larger organisations the conflict of objectives between shareholders and managers is more likely to occur. How can this be overcome?

Typically the manager should be aware if he is seen to underperform, he can be removed from office. Indeed directors are appointed by shareholders at periodic intervals to ensure that managers perform. In the case of listed companies managers also know that the company could be subject to a takeover bid. New owners are likely to review operations and to replace underperforming managers. Additionally the company could link the pay and remuneration of the manager to the financial performance of the business. By offering a bonus linked to profit targets, managers should be motivated to act in the interest of the shareholders. One problem here is that as we have seen, profits in the short term can be manipulated. Alternatively managers could be offered shares at favourable rates. Typically the manager would need to have a significant number of shares before he might be motivated in the desired way. Alternatively managers could be awarded share options. These allow the manager to purchase shares at an agreed price at a future date. Such options can encourage managers to act in ways that should have a positive impact on the share price. Over reliance on share options can however result in dysfunctional behaviour – as evidenced in some of the recent financial scandals. Finally the manager can be guided to act in the shareholder interest through the impact of the corporate governance system. Indeed the oversight and processes with which you will be familiar (independent non- executive directors, separation of the chairman and CEO roles and audit committees etc) are designed to encourage best practice with the aim of achieving the shareholder objectives.

A similar agency relationship exists between the management and the creditors. The management on behalf of the company borrow funds and from the lender point of view could take action which might prejudice their position. This can be overcome through the use of security and loan covenants as a means of overcoming the agency problem.

What are the links between finance and strategy?

The financial strategy plays a key factor in strategic success – in the sense that the successful management of the organisation's finances will determine the ability to generate funds to pay dividends, to create a pool of resources to enable the development of the business. The relationship between finance and strategy is captured by Johnson and Scholes 'Exploring Corporate Strategy' (Johnson + Scholes) in the following diagram:

The job of the chartered accountant as financial manager is concerned with:

- Meeting *the financial expectations* of the stakeholders in particular the shareholders. The dominant position of shareholders is a reflection of the fact that in a market economy shareholders, will sell their shares if they are not happy and this will impact on the future ability of the company to attract new funds. Equally should a company be seen to abuse its position with a bank (by being overdrawn without an approved overdraft facility) it will have difficulty in getting funds – or will only do so subject to additional restrictions or costs. You should refer to the discussion above on stakeholder perspectives. We have noted already how each of the various stakeholders will have different objectives and priorities.

- *Managing for value:* The financial manager will wish to manage the business in such a way that shareholder value is created. This could be achieved through:
  - ○ Increasing turnover or margin over time: This is likely to only be possible if we are offering a more valued proposition to the customer.
  - ○ Operating the business in such a way as to reduce costs perhaps through increased efficiencies or out-sourcing of activities.
  - ○ Reducing our investment in working capital or fixed assets. The former could be achieved by introducing a just-in-time stock system, the latter by a sale and leaseback.
  - ○ Shrewd selection of finance and the mix of alternative sources of finance (relying more on cheaper debt in place of equity) could enable a company to reduce its cost of capital.
  - ○ Management of our tax liabilities through careful tax planning could increase the funds available to shareholders.
  - ○ The creators of value are likely to centre on the successful investment in our brands, successful research and development and in our people development. The business needs to be managed in such a way as to enable sufficient funds to be available for this. A good example are the large pharmaceutical companies who use their patent protected 'blockbuster' drugs to generate strong cash flow which is used to fund their research and marketing efforts.
- *Funding strategies:* Selecting appropriate funds to support the strategic development of the business matching it to the needs of the investment and business needs in a way that does not create undue additional risks. Significant business expansion could create significant business requirements for finance requiring careful planning and negotiation including access to the financial markets (something you will cover later in the course).

A useful way to think of this is to see the business as a series of cash flows and if we maximise the present value of the cash flows we will be maximising shareholder wealth. This can be done by reducing our initial investment, (dispose of surplus assets, for example) improved working capital management, increasing our profits (increasing our prices and or reducing our costs) reducing our tax bill by careful tax planning and so on.

How might the organisation's financial position be evaluated?

The final part of this section deals with the evaluation of a company's position. In your earlier studies you have been introduced to the concept of ratio analysis as a way of identifying patterns and gaining insight into the company's performance. You should also draw on your knowledge of the 'big picture' strategic issues as a way of gaining insight.

Ratios can be categorised into four main categories:

- Profitability ratios
- Efficiency ratios
- Liquidity and gearing ratios
- Shareholder ratios.

Any analysis should consider a trend over a number of years as well as the characteristics of the industry in question. A further need is to consider how we are performing against any target that might have been set.

You should refer to Chapter 3 of your text, *Finance: Theory and Practice,* for a detailed review of ratio analysis and again attempt the relevant worked examples.

Appendix 2

Regulation of the Financial Services Industry

The work of a chartered accountant whether in practice or in industry, is affected and governed by the legislation governing industry generally (e.g. via the Companies Acts, Health and Safety Legislation and so on) as well as specific legislation governing the financial services industry. The legislation governing the financial services industry is required if investors are to have confidence in the safety of their investments. Over the last number of years there has been some concern expressed regarding the marketing practices of some financial institutions in the alleged mis-selling of insurance policies, for example, and this has resulted in greater regulation and oversight.

Key legislation

This section focuses primarily on the Financial Services Authority (FSA) applicable in the UK and the Irish Financial Services Regulatory Authority (IFSRA) in the Republic of Ireland, you should be aware of other relevant legislation as follows:

- Listing Rules (governing the issue of securities on a recognised exchange)
- City Code (governing takeovers etc);
- Companies Acts (governing issue of shares, shareholder rights, directors duties, repurchase of shares etc);
- Money laundering legislation;
- Professional codes of practice (issued by the Institute as well as other bodies such as the Banking profession etc).

The primary body governing the regulation of financial services within the UK is the Financial Services Authority (FSA). This is an independent, non-government body given statutory powers by the Financial Services and Markets Act 2000. It is funded by the financial services industry. Its four objectives are to:

1. maintain market confidence in the financial system;
2. promote public understanding of the financial system;
3. secure the appropriate degree of protection for consumers; and
4. reduce the extent to which it is possible for a business carried on by a regulated person to be used for purposes connected with financial crime.

The FSA must approve all firms or individuals before they can carry on a regulated activity. This means that the FSA will regulate and authorise all financial businesses, unit trusts, OEICs (open ended investment companies) and will recognise and supervise investment exchanges and clearing houses. In general terms all businesses involved in "investment business" require FSA authorisation this includes those dealing in investments (as principal or agent), arranging deals in investments, managing investments, advising investors on investments and so on. It means that all financial services industry falls under the FSA. The FSA carries out an assessment and ensures that all meet the necessary criteria to be eligible to engage in the regulated activity. The FSA has established ten principles which include that all firms should always act with due skills, care and diligence, observe high standards of integrity and fair dealing, avoid conflicts of interest, issue information in a timely and comprehensive manner etc.

In practice the FSA has sought to apply a level of flexibility in terms of the application of principles but it requires that those offering independent advice should not make any arrangements with other organisations in terms of gifts or inducements. All advertisements are subject to specific standards and they should take reasonable steps to ensure that the advise is appropriate to the individual's needs. Insider dealing (i.e. trading in investments using "inside information) is illegal.

The FSA supervises the prudential soundness of banks and building societies. It also supervises all insurers. In addition to regulating investment firms (covering investment banks, stockbrokers, independent financial advisors and corporate finance practitioners) it also regulates lawyers and accountants who undertake investment business. Professional firms who have incidental investment business and meet certain criteria are 'exempt professional firms' and can undertake some regulated activities under supervision by their designated professional body. Examples of designated professional bodies include:

- The Institute of Chartered Accountants in Ireland (ICAI)
- The Institute Chartered Accountants of Scotland
- The Association of Chartered Certified Accountants
- The Institute of Actuaries
- The Institute of Chartered Accountants in England and Wales
- The Law Society

All chartered accountant firms authorised by the ICAI to carry on investment business are required to comply with the ICAI regulations in this area and in turn are subject to regulation by the Institute.

The FSA investigates, and where appropriate, disciplines and or prosecutes those responsible for breaking the rules. It works closely with criminal authorities and has both criminal and civil powers. Amongst other things it has power to:

- Withdraw a firm's authorisation
- Discipline firms and individuals approved by the FSA

- Impose fines for market abuse
- Prosecute for various offences, and
- Require the return of money to compensate consumers.

The FSA aims to promote public understanding of the financial system and protect consumers. It promotes public understanding through providing financial education in schools, publishing comparative tables of products, providing a consumer help line and publishing financial information in the form of fact sheets.

Financial crimes are also prohibited and cover such illegal acts as:

- *Manipulation of the market* for example by spreading false statements or rumours or abusing a dominant position resulting perhaps in the manipulation of share prices. At the time of writing the financial regulator in the Republic is examining trading records of various stockbrokers looking for possible manipulation of bank share prices.
- *Money laundering* (i.e. the processing of funds from illegal activities such as crime, drug dealing etc), is specifically prohibited. Strict measures are now in place to ensure that banks and financial intermediaries can provide details of the sources of funds that are received. This also puts an onus on financial institution when an account is being opened to ensure that the account holder is a legal person and not just a 'front' for a criminal! Chartered accountants in practice have also to take care that they comply with this regulations.

Regulations governing listed companies

At the CAP 1 finance course the focus was on the financial needs of small entities which typically might rely on bank finance, venture capital and so on. As companies develop they may wish to raise funds via the stock exchange. There are specific rules and regulations in place governing this area. In London there are two markets, the Official List (main market) and the Alternative Investment Market (AIM). A company is said to be listed only if it trades on the main market (rather than the AIM). The equivalent in Dublin is the Irish stock exchange and the Irish Enterprise Exchange and the Alternative Securities Market.

To have one's shares listed on the official list one must satisfy two criteria:

- The listing rules must be satisfied (often referred to as the Purple Book). This details the specific regulatory requirements that must be met to list on the market.
- The company will also need to apply to the exchange to have its shares listed.

The listing rules cover:

- Chapter 1 states the rules regarding the compliance with, and enforcement of, the listing rules and the sanctions for breaching them.
- Chapters 2 to 8 deal with the various documents that are needed to deal with an application for listing.
- Chapters 9 to 16 deal with the continuing obligations for listed companies.
- Chapters 17 to 27 deal with specialised areas such as property companies etc.

These requirements are dealt with in more detail your text and in the web links below.

Web supports:

Further resources and information are at:

London Stock Exchange website: http://www.londonstockexchange.com

Irish Stock Exchange Website: http://www.ise.ie

Financial Services Authority website: http://www.fsa.gov.uk/

IFSRA website (the financial regulator): http://www.ifsra.ie/

ICAI website for support on investment business: http://www.icai.ie/Members/memb-auditinvst.cfm

Applications for a Listing

The company will need to be a plc, normally with three years of published audited accounts. The securities (shares, preference shares etc) to be listed must conform with the law of the place of incorporation, the whole class must be admitted to trading and the securities must be freely transferable.

The securities must have a market capitalisation of at least £700,000 for shares and £200,000 for debt securities. 25% of the shares must be in the hands of the public.

The AIM (or in the case of the Republic the IEX) are designed for smaller companies and the requirements and costs are much less strict. For example there is no minimum trading record, nor limits on the market capitalisation. Admission on these exchanges is often a stepping stone to a full listing later on.

You should recall from your study of company law that there are specific requirements governing the issue of shares including requirements governing prospectuses and their contents. For listed companies these requirements are more significant and are detailed in Chapter 6 of the Listing Rules. Commonly where shares are being issued, a reporting accountant (typically an auditor) will be involved and will report on the accuracy of the information filed on support of the application for listing. There are specific requirements where profit forecasts are included and the reporting accountant (or auditor) will be required to confirm that it has been properly compiled and is consistent with the company's accounting policies.

Once a company is listed there are ongoing requirements which must be met including restrictions on when directors and others can trade in shares, requirements to publish interim results (every six months) and to make announcements when certain transactions arise – the latter seek to keep an orderly market at all times.

City Code

All listed companies are required to comply with the City Code on Takeovers and Mergers. The code has no legal backing although the Takeover Panel enforces it. All public companies (whether listed or unlisted) must comply with the code. The code seeks to ensure that all shareholders are treated equally, information is adequately disclosed and that the board of directors of the target company do not try and thwart the takeover without the approval of its shareholders. The code also contains detailed rules which govern a takeover including rules on:

- How to approach target companies;
- The timing of share purchases;

- The announcement of a takeover bid;
- The obligation of the board of a target company to seek independent advice; and
- Conduct during the offer.

The Takeover Panel cannot reverse what has happened nor impose a sanction after the event. It can however change the rules to ensure unfair practices cannot happen again.

Additionally, should a takeover involve a company acquiring a dominant position in the market place any takeover can be referred to the Competition Commission which has powers to block takeovers or to permit them subject to significant conditions (e.g. the disposal of significant part of the business). In certain circumstances the European Commission have to approve significant takeovers – or indeed can block these as in the case of the Ryanair bid for Aer Lingus.

In summary there are extensive rules and regulations which govern this area and a chartered accountant in the various roles that can be held, (financial director, reporting accountant, auditor etc) must comply with these regulations.

TOPIC TWO
INVESTMENT DECISIONS, FINANCING DECISIONS AND DISTRIBUTION DECISIONS

INVESTMENT DECISIONS, FINANCING DECISIONS AND DISTRIBUTION DECISIONS

We will now move onto the second topic on the course; Investment Decisions, Financing Decisions and Distribution Decisions.

Topic 2: Investment, Financing and Distribution Decisions   **Weighting:** 30%

Objective: To demonstrate an ability to assess all financing aspects of a medium to large organisation with a particular emphasis on external (listing and equivalent) sources and advise on distributions and mergers and acquisitions

Learning Outcomes

Completion of this course enables the student to:

- Be able to identify short, medium and long term financial requirements bearing in mind the particular circumstances and to prepare a financing plan
- Advise on the process of raising capital externally with an emphasis on stock exchange or equivalent external sources.
- Advise on dividend policy
- Advise on and perform appropriate valuations for M&A investments and recommend financing alternatives. Highlight due diligence issues. Appreciate the broader context of these activities.
- Identify or advise financially troubled businesses and formulate options for simple reconstructions

---

28 STRATEGIC FINANCE AND MANAGEMENT ACCOUNTING TOOLKIT

Later that week you receive the following e-mail from Harry with a number of attachments.

To: jamescrowm@sonner&saville.com

From: harryoneill@sonner&saville.com

Re: IBRT Ltd

James,

I hope that you are beginning to settle into your new role and are looking forward to the challenges ahead of you. Over the next number of months one of our larger sized clients, IBRT Ltd will be looking to expand its markets, and is looking at how it will finance this expansion as well as ways to manage the resulting risks. IBRT Ltd has up to now traded exclusively in Ireland / the UK in the manufacturing sector.

Some of the key contacts that you will meet are Mary Patterson who is the Chairman of the Board of IBRT Ltd and Patrick Murphy who is the Finance Director. IBRT Ltd has always operated as an independent company, developing its interests in its chosen field by building up its own skill base. This certainly suited the organisation when it was founded in the 1970's by Mary's father Peter Patterson, but after Peter passed away a few years ago, the company's ownership was split between Mary, her two brothers, 6 grandchildren and a number of private equity investors. In addition, the company has been expanding over the last number of years and this has added to the size and nature of the issues it faces.

The most recent Balance Sheet and Income Statement information for IBRT Ltd is attached. Over the next number of weeks I will be working quite closely with Patrick and Mary and will expect you to assist me in meeting their requirements.

Regards,

Harry

Balance Sheet of IBRT Ltd as at 31 December 2008

		€/£M's	€/£M's	€/£M's
Land & Buildings			100	
Plant & Equipment			25	125
Other Investments			30	
Goodwill			20	50
Current Assets:	Inventory	10		
	Cash	8		
	Debtors	25	43	
Current Liabilities:	Trade Creditors	(12)		
	Bank Overdraft	(17)	(29)	14
				189

Represented By:

	€/£M's	€/£M's
Share Capital – issued shares of €/£0.50 each	10	
Retained Earnings	129	139
Debenture Stock		50
		189

In addition, profits after taxation and dividends for the last five years are as follows:

	Profit after €/£Ms'	Tax Dividends €/£Ms'
Year ended December 31st 2008	35	10*
Year ended December 31st 2007	32	9
Year ended December 31st 2006	37	10
Year ended December 31st 2005	28	8
Year ended December 31st 2004	22	6

* The 2008 dividend has yet to be declared. This is a best estimate of the proposed dividend

STRATEGIC FINANCE AND MANAGEMENT ACCOUNTING TOOLKIT

You meet Harry in the corridor on the way back from the canteen and he asks you to step into his office for a few minutes.

Patrick Murphy has been on the phone to him in relation to some discussions that were being held at Board level of IBRT Ltd. A question came up from one of the Directors in relation to the liquidity of the shares within IBRT Ltd. An issue arose as to whether IBRT Ltd should consider a listing on the Stock Market which would in turn allow for a greater market in their shares. As a result of this, Patrick has asked Harry to call to the head office of IBRT Ltd the following day in order to brief him on the options and associated issues.

As this seems quite a big task, Harry will break it into precise chunks of work and will ask you to cover off some areas. As an initial exercise he has asked you to inform him in relation to the various advantages and disadvantages for IBRT Ltd of having a Stock Market quotation. This would form the basic building block of any advice that he would be passing onto IBRT Ltd. Before attempting to complete tasks 5 to 7 you need to study **Chapter 7** of your text and attempt questions 1 to 2.

> **Task 5: Prepare an e-mail for Harry outlining the advantages and disadvantages of having a stock market quotation.**

Harry received the mail and complimented you on the content. As a next step he asks you to look at the markets that would be available to IBRT Ltd in the UK and The Republic of Ireland. He also asks you to advise on what initial requirements would need to be met to ensure a listing is obtained, and what are the ongoing reporting requirements of the various exchanges.

> **Task 6: Prepare a memorandum outlining the various Stock Exchanges in The Republic of Ireland and the UK as well as their initial and ongoing reporting requirements.**

Having reviewed the memorandum, Harry is pleasantly surprised with the amount of detail that you have been able to pull together for him in a short space of time. He had been planning to assign another task

INVESTMENT DECISIONS, FINANCING DECISIONS AND DISTRIBUTION DECISIONS 31

to Derek. However Derek was called away at short notice to an audit in another part of the city, so Harry asked if you would do another task for him. One question that Patrick had raised as a matter for IBRT Ltd's Board to consider was the method of share issue. Patrick was aware that there were various types and he wanted to be informed of the options available.

> **Task 7: Prepare a brief e-mail to Harry outlining the various types of share issues available to IBRT Ltd and explain any related factors that should be considered.**

Patrick has been on the phone again to Harry who subsequently calls you into the office. Now that the 2008 year-end has been completed, IBRT Ltd is in the process of declaring a dividend for the year. As far as you can gather there appears to be some disquiet within the company as to what the actual level of the dividend payout should be. In the past, dividends have been approximately 2/7ths of distributable income. Some of the Board members who are shareholders appear to derive a significant portion of their personal income from the annual dividends and have been arguing for a greater dividend. On the other hand, a number of the other shareholders on the Board are independently wealthy and would rather see the money reinvested in the company to fund future growth and increase overall company value.

Patrick asks Harry to prepare a brief for him in terms of formulating a dividend policy in general. He is quite nervous about the meeting with the Board as he knows that some will have differing views. Harry passes on this request to you. Before attempting to complete tasks 8 and 9 you need to study **Chapter 19** of your text and attempt questions 1 to 6.

> **Task 8: Outline for Harry the main considerations a company will take account of in formulating a dividend policy.**

Some days later Harry calls you into the office. He has just heard back from Patrick that the Board meeting went better than expected and that Patrick was very grateful for the information that Sonner & Saville had provided to him. IBRT Ltd is going to declare a dividend of €/£10M for the financial year 2008. However there was some degree of disgruntlement at the meeting. One of the shareholders asked if there was any other way in which they could get returns for the investment that they were making. She specifically mentioned the possibility of a share repurchase. Patrick was asked to go and investigate the feasibility of doing this and to report back to the Board in a couple of days. He passed the request onto Harry who immediately turned it over to you, and asked you to prepare a brief to go directly to Patrick as he would be gone away.

> **Task 9: Outline by e-mail the other types of distributions that can be made by IBRT Ltd in respect of their shareholder base including the possibility of a share repurchase.**

The following week Harry is back in the office. He calls you in and asks you to shut the door of his office. You are a bit surprised as Harry has a reputation of being one of the most approachable people in the office and this lends an air of trepidation to your demeanour. However he puts you at ease immediately by saying that he has a challenge for you that should make your job a whole lot more interesting and will make you the envy of your peer group. Not quite sure how to take this, you ask him to explain a little more. He says that he has been contacted by Patrick and Mary in relation to an approach by another Irish/UK Company (Jones Bros Ltd) to acquire IBRT Ltd.

It is obvious from how he is approaching the discussion that Harry does not want to go into a huge amount of detail. However reading between the lines you get the impression that one or more of the family may want out for whatever reasons.

Harry is in the process of requesting some financial information from Patrick and Mary in relation to IBRT Ltd, and said that he will also try and get his hands on similar information in relation to Jones Bros Ltd. He asks you to read up on the whole area of Mergers and Acquisitions overnight and to get ready for a busy few weeks! Suitably motivated, you decide that this will not be a night for the cinema and you go home with some files, some reading material, a jar of coffee, some biscuits and prepare to brief yourself. Before attempting to complete

INVESTMENT DECISIONS, FINANCING DECISIONS AND DISTRIBUTION DECISIONS   33

tasks 10-19 you need to study **Chapter 17** of your text and attempt questions 1 to 4.

> **Task 10: Outline the main causes and motives for Merger and Acquisition activity.**

The following morning you have read up on the main reasons for mergers and acquisitions. Though a bit bleary eyed you pop into Harry's office and explain to him that you are ready for whatever needs to be done next. Suitably impressed, Harry gets Patrick on the line and a brief discussion ensues. Patrick has an urgent request. Jones Bros are going to call him at 11.00 am and ask him about performing due diligence on the books of IBRT Ltd. Patrick asks that Harry sends him an e-mail within the next hour highlighting the key areas that he might expect Jones Bros to request information on. That way he feels he can better prepare for the call in the short time span available to him. With a clear mandate to dispense with any formalities, Harry asks you to send him a mail by 10.15 a.m. that he can in turn pass onto Patrick.

You talk with Harry for a few minutes and he suggests that you speak to John Keane who is the audit partner in Sonner & Saville and to a couple of his staff who may also have some ideas. Time is of the essence so you do not delay.

> **Task 11: Prepare a brief e-mail to Harry outlining the main areas that he can expect Jones Bros to look at in terms of performing a due diligence of IBRT Ltd.**

Following receipt of the mail and the subsequent telephone conversation with Jones Bros Ltd, Patrick agreed that the due diligence would take place once the Board had met. In the meantime he was able to forward to Harry some relevant financial information in relation to the Balance Sheet and Income Statement of IBRT Ltd:

(i)   The 'Other Investments' figure represents a 20% stake in an electronics company. IBRT Ltd has recently received an offer for this stake of €/£50M, which it has not accepted as it believes the

34 STRATEGIC FINANCE AND MANAGEMENT ACCOUNTING TOOLKIT

company will be floated on the stock exchange later in the year with a total market capitalisation of €/£400M.

(ii) The figure for land and buildings includes €/£30M in respect of IBRT Ltd's headquarters, which IBRT believes will not be needed if the acquisition goes ahead. IBRT have had a number of approaches from other companies interested in the property and believe they could sell this for at least €/£100M.

(iii) The debenture stockholders have agreed in principle with IBRT to have their debenture stock redeemed at a total cost of €/£55M in the event of any takeover.

(iv) If the acquisition were to take place, IBRT Ltd knows it is the intention of Jones Bros Ltd to undertake a major rationalisation plan. This plan will result in up-front costs of €/£50M being incurred after tax but would result in an increase in after-tax profits of €/£10M p.a.

(v) Two other companies with businesses similar to IBRT are already quoted on the stock exchange and the data relating to them is as follows:

	P/E Ratio
Lomu Ltd	11
Elwood Ltd	9

(vi) Of the year-end debtors balance, it is believed that €/£4M will turn out to be a bad debt.

(vii) The purchase of IBRT Ltd should allow Jones Bros Ltd to realise operational savings due to the benefits of synergy of €/£8M p.a. before tax. However, one division of IBRT which earns after tax profits of €/£4M p.a. would have to be closed, with associated redundancy costs of €/£3M after tax.

(vii) Jones Bros Ltd has a required rate of return of 18%.

Given this information, Patrick asked if you and Harry could look at coming up with a possible price range for the shares in IBRT Ltd to evaluate any offer that Jones Bros might make after performing their due diligence. Before attempting to complete task 12 you need to study **Chapter 17** of your text and attempt questions 1 to 3.

INVESTMENT DECISIONS, FINANCING DECISIONS AND DISTRIBUTION DECISIONS   35

Task 12: Using the above information and assuming a rate of corporation tax of 12.5%, come up with a possible price range for the Shares in IBRT Ltd.

Having passed on the information to Patrick, Harry gets an interesting phone call from Mary Patterson. It appears that the imminent approach from Jones Bros has begun to unnerve Mary slightly. While she is still going to allow due diligence to take place, she is feeling a bit guilty about selling the company that her late father had spent so many years building up. She has asked Harry for some detail as to the steps that IBRT Ltd might take to make the takeover less attractive if that was a course of action that she wished to pursue. She impressed upon Harry the confidential nature of her request, which he likewise stressed to you. Harry asked you to research this topic and come up with some ideas that could be useful, should Mary decide to try and resist the approach from IBRT Ltd.

Task 13: Prepare a memorandum for Harry detailing the most common steps that could be undertaken by an organisation in resisting a takeover bid.

It is obvious that Mary Patterson is seriously looking at what she is going to do in relation to the possible takeover of IBRT Ltd. She calls Harry back and drops into the office for a confidential chat. A good discussion takes place around the pros and cons of the various defences against the possible takeover by Jones Bros. Harry is a bit mystified as to why Patrick is not also at the meeting, but this becomes clear when Mary moves the discussion onto another topic. Apparently, when Mary's father died, not only did he leave IBRT Ltd as a successfully established company, but he also had a number of other investments which he had divided out among the family members.

One such investment was that of Giles Ltd, a property development company based in the city, but operating in the Republic of Ireland and the UK, with some penetration into overseas property markets, most notably in Spain, Portugal and Bulgaria. The company had been quite successful throughout the 1990's and the early part of the millennium, but in recent years some of their investments had began to look less attractive to customers. The company's policy had been to use debt to finance their acquisition of property. Due to a slow down in sales in the previous two years, they have been left with a substantial amount of debt on their balance sheet and have experienced a write down in the value of their properties. Mary has been a board member of Giles Ltd for the last seven years and has a 3% stake in the company. A Board meeting is called for the following Saturday, and Mary feels that she needs to do some preparation work for the meeting as the company's future is up for discussion.

She provides you with the following summary extracts from the Financial Accounts of Giles Ltd. She has asked that Sonner & Saville do an analysis of the information that is currently available. She will pass on more information as it becomes available to her.

Giles Ltd
Balance Sheet

	31.12.07 Actual €/£ Ms	31.12.08 Actual €/£ Ms	31.03.09 Projected €/£ Ms
Non Current Assets			
Land & Buildings	500	500	500
Plant and machinery	150	190	330
	650	690	830
Current Assets			
Inventory	650	1,000	1,100
Debtors	50	60	70
	700	1,060	1,170
Current Liabilities			
Trade Creditors	260	400	500
Bank overdraft (unsecured)	–	400	570
	260	800	1,070

Net Current Assets	440	260	100
Total Assets Less Current Liabilities	1,090	950	930
Long Term Liabilities	–		
10% debentures 2010			
(secured on Land & Buildings)	(100)	(100)	(100)
Other loans (floating charges)	–	(100)	(120)
	990	750	710
Financed By:			
Ordinary shares of €/£1	750	750	750
8% Cumulative preference shares	200	200	200
Accumulated reserves/ (deficit)	40	(200)	(240)
	990	750	710

> ### Task 14: Prepare a brief memorandum for Mary analysing the financial position of Giles Ltd.

Mary receives the information on Wednesday as agreed, and she has scheduled a meeting with some of the other shareholders in the bank on Friday before the board meeting that is set for Saturday. She understands that your analysis is based on partial information but she is experiencing some difficulty in getting the exact details you require. However, armed with your request, she asks the company's Finance Director to attend the meeting and she receives some more information. On Wednesday night, Mary e-mails you some of the critical data that you were looking for in relation to the Income Statement performance for the last number of accounting periods, and this should allow you to complete the analysis. This is attached.

Giles Ltd

Income Statement for Accounting period ended

	31.12.07	31.12.08	31.03.09
	12Mth Actual	12Mth Actual	3Mth Projtd
	€/£Ms	€/£Ms	€/£Ms
Gross Profit			
Sales	2,000	1,700	350
Cost Of Sales	(1,660)	(1,600)	(290)
Gross profit	340	100	60
Other Expenses			
Interest	0	120	50
Administration costs	200	160	30
Depreciation	30	10	10
General Expenses	90	50	10
Net Profit / (Loss)	20	(240)	(40)
Opening Retained Earnings Balance	20	40	(200)
Closing Retained Earnings Reserve Balance	40	(200)	(240)

> **Task 15: Given the additional information provided by Mary Patterson, please adjust your original memorandum to take account of the new facts.**

Following the Board meeting you get a call from Harry on Saturday morning. He apologises for calling you at the weekend, but as Mary is one of his most important clients he says that he is honour bound to help her and time may be at a premium. He asks if you can be in the office for 11.00 a.m. as there is some critical analysis that you will need to do for Mary by tomorrow morning. This is not an issue for you, as you know that Harry would not call you in on a Saturday unless it was urgent. Anyway, you are getting great experience and you know that when things are quiet in the office you can often finish early, so it has to work both ways.

Upon arriving in the office, Harry immediately shows you a number of documents that Mary has given him. They contain various disjointed pieces of information concerning the cash flow position of Giles Ltd. over the next couple of years. As far as you can gather, the discussion at the Board meeting was fairly heated. The two main lending institutions that had advanced money to Giles Ltd. in the last couple of years were extremely worried about the company's ability to repay the money that they had lent, not to mention the interest payments necessary to service the debt. Both banks had members on the board of Giles Ltd. The preference shareholders were also angry about not receiving a dividend payment for the last three years. As they did not have voting rights in the company, they were feeling very frustrated. Equally, those board members who were also ordinary shareholders were worried that their investment in the company was worthless at this stage.

During the discussion various options were considered but the one that caused the most emotion was from one of the financial institutions who were clearly anxious to cut their losses and wind up the company. This certainly appeared to have raised the temperature at the meeting, resulting in a protracted discussion as to the merits or otherwise of taking this action. Mary was viewed by all sides as an honest broker. Although a shareholder, she did not really take a huge amount of interest in the company and did not have any executive powers, and hence she had no emotional attachment to the company. When the meeting appeared to have reached an impasse, she stepped in and agreed that she would work with the parties to ascertain the financial situation should the company be wound up.

Following discussion through the night, Mary obtained the following pieces of information which she felt would be relevant. She passed these onto Harry in the morning, hence his call to you. Harry detailed the information as follows;

- The land and buildings had not been independently valued for over six years and it was felt that, given the current location of the company's offices, they were worth at least €/£550M.

STRATEGIC FINANCE AND MANAGEMENT ACCOUNTING TOOLKIT

- While the plant and machinery owned by the company was relatively new, given the current downturn in the construction sector it was felt that it would only realise €/£70M if sold on the open market.
- The value of the company's housing stock had already been reassessed in the prior year, but the company reckoned that the current market value of their inventory was only €/£600M.
- It was estimated that approximately €/£30M of the Debtors would be recoverable in a liquidation situation, while Trade Creditors were accurately valued at present.
- Were the company to go into liquidation it would cost approximately €/£100M in administration costs.

> **Task 16: Using the above information prepare a summary of the cash position and who would get what if the company were to be wound up on the 31st March 2009.**

As well as providing details in relation to a liquidation situation, Mary was able to get her hands on some additional information during the day. She has provided you with the expected cash flows for the next 5 accounting periods, should Giles Ltd stay in business.

This information is attached below:

	9 Months to	Years ending 31st December			
	31.12.09	2010	2011	2012	2013
	€/£ M	€/£ M	€/£ M	€/£ M	€/£ M
Receipts from sales	1300	1600	1800	2000	2400
Payments to suppliers	(1000)	(1200)	(1350)	(1450)	(1760)
Purchase of equipment	(40)	(70)	(10)	(50)	(80)
Other expenses	(110)	(190)	(170)	(180)	(180)
Interest charges	(180)	(200)	(220)	(200)	(180)
Net Receipts/ (Expenditure)	(30)	(60)	50	120	200

The above figures are based on the assumption that the present capital structure is maintained.

INVESTMENT DECISIONS, FINANCING DECISIONS AND DISTRIBUTION DECISIONS 41

Given the result of the analysis that you completed under the previous task, Mary is interested in seeing if it is worth keeping the company trading, and whether this might be a better option

> **Task 17: Using the information provided, prepare an analysis of the future funding required to keep Giles Ltd trading, and what the benefit of doing so might be for the ordinary shareholders.**

Following your analysis, Mary is quite enthused about the prospect of Giles Ltd continuing to trade. Harry says that, in reality, this is a situation that Mary would like to ensure happens, if for no other reason than the fact that she would like to keep the legacy of her father's involvement with Giles Ltd going. Apparently it was one of the first companies that he was involved in, and therefore one that was close to his heart.

Following some discussions with the board again on Monday morning, it was decided that the company would be better off if it continued to trade. A scheme of reconstruction was called for. Mary undertook to speak formally with Sonner & Saville in relation to this scheme. One of the prerequisites that was outlined by the Board was that no scheme should be proposed that would leave any of the parties to the scheme worse off than if the company were to be wound up.

Harry, Mary and you were asked to identify what the current parties would get if the company was wound up now, and to use this as a starting point to come up with a proposed scheme of reconstruction.

> **Task 18: Given the requirement that no party should be worse off than they are at present, suggest a reconstruction scheme that would enable the company to continue to trade.**

Mary is delighted with the outcome of the discussions and she takes this to the next meeting of the Board. While there is indeed a lot of discussion as to the viability of the entity going forward, the conciseness of the plan and its obvious merit are enough to sway all the Board members. More importantly, the two lending institutions and creditors also appear to be happy with the proposals and therefore it is a runner.

Harry is delighted as Sonner & Saville come in for some well earned praise. He promises that he will make up for your lost weekend during the summer months, when the office is a lot quieter. As a final request, Mary has asked that Sonner & Saville prepare a detailed document showing how the company will perform financially following the scheme of reconstruction.

Harry asks you to prepare a response to this request as soon as possible.

> **Task 19: Detail how the reconstructed company will perform once the reconstruction takes place, and whether or not the reconstructed company will be financially viable.**

The discussion with Mary has concentrated on the reconstruction of the company, and has focused on retaining the current sources of finance and just re-jigging the amount provided by each. Therefore, while Giles Ltd is renegotiating the amount provided by the bank overdraft, the long term loans and debentures, Mary is unsure as to the appropriateness of these as sources of finance. Similarly, in terms of the equity funding, Mary's focus has been on the existing ordinary and preference shareholders, and she had not looked at what other alternative sources of equity finance might be available. Mary has spoken with Harry and requested that Sonner & Saville prepare a brief memorandum, identifying some of the characteristics of the sources of finance currently being used, and whether there might be other suitable sources available to Giles Ltd. Before attempting to carry out Task 20, you should study **Chapters 4 to 7** of the text.

> **Task 20: Briefly list the characteristics of the sources of finance already being used by Giles Ltd, and identify any other sources of finance that might be suitable.**

Following all of this discussion Mary is aware that her father has left her a number of investments in different companies across the Republic of

Ireland and the UK. As a result of this, and the fact that she has had to have an active involvement in Giles Ltd, during recent weeks, she has asked if Sonner & Saville can provide her with a briefing in relation to business failure. In particular, she is interested in the main causes of business failure and any indicators that can be used in order to identify failure at an early stage, so that something can be done to prevent it occurring.

> **Task 21: Prepare a memorandum for Harry that he can pass onto Mary Patterson, detailing the main causes of business failure and the early warning signs that can be used to identify the likelihood of such failures occurring.**

TOPIC THREE
RISK DECISIONS

RISK DECISIONS

We will now move onto the third topic of the Competency Statement, Risk Decisions.

Topic 3: Risk Decisions   **Weighting:**   20%

Objective: To demonstrate an ability to identify and use alternative methods of managing risk exposures such as currency and interest risks

Learning Outcomes

Completion of this course enables the student to:

- Advise on alternatives of a centralised and decentralised treasury function and how it may be evaluated
- Advise on risk management strategies:
  - Identify and evaluate the key financial risks facing a business and show how it can be managed and measured
  - Outline how a risk management policy may be set and how it is monitored distinguishing different risk attitudes
  - Explain different methods of managing currency and interest rate risks appropriate to a given situation, performing simple calculations to determine the cost and choice of the hedge
  - Determine the financial implications of a derivative position

Harry calls you into his office and asks you to sit down. He says that he has some interesting work that he needs you to do for him. IBRT Ltd are now looking at opportunities to expand and before they do so they are looking at the risk associated with their company. As a result Harry asks you to look at the whole area of risk management and provide him with some documentation on this area that he can use. Before you carry out tasks 22 to 24 you will need to read the Introduction to Chapter 18 of your text as well as the section on Managing Risk.

> **Task 22: Prepare a brief memorandum to Harry outlining what is meant by risk management.**

Harry thanked you for your memorandum and indicated that this was something that he would like you to do some research on in the next number of days. Patrick had two informational requirements in relation to risk that Harry needed to come back to him on. The first was to prepare a brief summary on the high level risks that IBRT Ltd might face as a company and the second was around risk management … what constitutes risk management and what could a company do to manage their risks at a high level?

> **Task 23: Prepare an e-mail to Harry detailing the different types of risks that can face an organisation.**

> **Task 24: Prepare an e-mail to Harry detailing how IBRT Ltd can put in place a risk management policy to identify, assess and address these risks.**

Patrick was delighted with the information that Harry provided for him. Patrick told Harry that IBRT Ltd was looking at a number of expansion opportunities that might arise over the next number of months. Interestingly, Patrick had said to Harry that while IBRT Ltd currently traded in The Republic of Ireland / Northern Ireland and managed its own finances from its headquarters in the city, Patrick was still interested in learning more about what the Treasury function in a company should manage, and the advantages of having a centralised treasury function. Harry asked you to look at this and send him a memorandum on this topic so he could inform Patrick. Before you complete this task you will need to read up on the Treasury Function section in **Chapter 19** of your text.

> **Task 25: Prepare a memorandum to Harry listing the things a Treasury Department in an organisation should manage and the advantages of having a centralised Treasury function.**

Patrick telephones to look for some advice. Due to work that has been done by the IBRT Marketing Department he feels that the possibility of trading outside of the Republic of Ireland / UK is imminent. However this would be a first for Patrick and he needs some guidance as to the different types of currency risk that exist and what is meant by these. You talk with Harry and he asks you to prepare a brief memorandum for Patrick explaining the different types of currency risk. Harry also asks you to read up on some other material which will help to inform your memorandum. Harry is excited about this request, as he believes that it may be the start of a growth phase in IBRT Ltd which could create opportunities for the services of Sonner & Saville. Before you complete tasks 26 to 31 you will need to read up on the Managing Risk and Exchange Rate Risk sections in **Chapter 18** of your text. In addition you should attempt questions 1 to 5 and question 7 in the text.

> **Task 26: Prepare a brief memorandum to Patrick outlining the different types of currency risk faced by organisations that trade internationally.**

Harry calls you into his office and says he is just off the phone from Patrick. The memorandum that you wrote went down well, and Harry was interested in retaining Sonner & Saville to provide advice on its foreign currency transactions. As it turns out, IBRT Ltd had, that afternoon, made a sale of 50 products to a US company based in Boston for a total consideration of $100,000. The goods would be finished in the factory by the 15th of March, and, as usual with IBRT Ltd, 30 days credit from date of shipment have been given with the sale.

This is an exciting development for IBRT Ltd, as it marks the result of some work they have been doing with a number of trade delegations to the US in the previous six months. As this is the company's first venture into a foreign market, they have looked for some advice as to how then can handle the deal. The price on the contract was set following an e-procurement on-line auction, in which IBRT Ltd beat off some strong competition from the US and International based companies. However, because the price was so competitive, Patrick is worried that any adverse movements in exchange rate will impact on the profitability of the sale. Given the reluctance that he faced internally within the company in terms of expanding its operations abroad, he does not want this to occur.

He has approached his current bank to enquire as to possible ways that he can reduce this risk. One way that has been suggested to him is to enter into a forward contract so that he can sell his $100,000 to the bank in one month's time. The rate quoted by his bank for doing this is $1.60 to €/£1.00. Patrick is unsure as to whether this represents good value or not, and has turned to you for your advice.

You are aware that Forward Contract rates depend very much on the current spot rate and interest rates. Therefore you look up a number of newspapers and discover that the current rate of interest on US Deposits is 4% and it is only 3% in the Republic of Ireland / UK. In addition, if you were to walk in off the high street today, you could get a spot rate of $1.57 to €/£1.00.

> **Task 27: Advise Patrick as to whether he has been offered a good forward contract rate of exchange, or whether he should be looking elsewhere for a better rate.**

Following your analysis Patrick decides not to proceed with the Forward Contract with his existing bank. However, he is still conscious of the fact that Foreign Exchange rates are extremely volatile at present, and he does not want to take the chance that his anticipated profit margin on the sale will be eroded by Foreign Exchange rate movements. He is looking for your advice in relation to other alternatives he may have.

RISK DECISIONS 51

You approach Harry at this stage and talk to him about this. He says that he will be able to offer you some high level guidance in terms of identifying the possible ways the exposure can be managed, but that you will need to work out the actual details yourself. The first way he suggests that you can manage the exposure is to look at using the money markets.

In this scenario, he says that Patrick can hedge against the currency exchange risk by borrowing a certain amount of USD now so that when the interest on the loan for one month is added, it will equate to $100,000 on 15th April. The $100,000 that IBRT Ltd will receive from it's customer on April 15th will then be used to pay off the USD loan at that date. Meanwhile, the USD borrowed now can be translated into Euros / Sterling on March 15th.

He sends you off to investigate this alternative and asks you to come back to him with your findings. You realise from looking at the Financial Times that the current USD lending rate is 8%.

> **Task 28: Advise Patrick as to the outcome if he chooses to hedge IBRT Ltd's risk by using the money market.**

When you call back, Patrick is much happier with the result of this calculation. He is however worried about transaction costs and has asked you to look at some other alternatives that might be available to him in terms of managing this exposure.

You are conscious that the March 15th date is drawing closer and that the product is already moving along the production floor of IBRT Ltd. Therefore you again approach Harry and ask him about the other choices that may be available to IBRT Ltd. He suggests that you explore the possibility of using a currency option. You are not quite sure what he means by this so he does a little bit of investigation for you.

Harry calls you about 10 minutes later and says that he has been in touch with a friend of his in a bank who will call you back with some information. Later you receive a phone call from Fiona who works with First Bank PLC. She is a currency trader and knows Harry from their college days. After sharing some banter about the Rugby match the previous weekend, Fiona informs you that she can sell you a currency option to sell $100,000 at a rate of \$1.56 to €1/£1. However there will be a fee associated with this that she will need to work out.

When you talk to Patrick he quite likes the idea of the currency option. The big advantage for him is that IBRT will gain if the exchange rate weakens. However if the USD strengthens beyond \$1.56 to €/£1.00, IBRT Ltd has the alternative of not taking up the option and of benefiting from the better exchange rate. He asks you to advise him on the attractiveness (or not) of the option.

> **Task 29: Advise Patrick as to the outcome if he chooses the option contract. Work out the maximum he should be prepared to pay First Bank PLC for this option, given the alternative worked out with the money market.**

Following this analysis Patrick asks you if it would be possible to use Currency Futures to manage his exposure. You are not entirely sure how this would work so you head into Harry again to assist you. Harry explains that Futures are a form of forward contract which can be traded on a futures market, where standardised future contracts can be bought in anticipation of a foreign payment being needed, and then closed out on the payment date. Harry admits that this too is an area that he is not quite familiar with, and he proceeds to make some phone calls. He eventually makes contact with a former colleague of his, John O'Toole, from a city centre practice. John informs Harry that Futures trade in blocks of \$10,000 each. John says that it would be possible to arrange to sell futures on March 15th, and buy on April 15th (i.e., when the proceeds of the sale arrive).

> **Task 30: Advise Patrick as to how using futures might assist him.**

John also said that there was another possibility that might be open to IBRT Ltd. One of his clients is a US Multi-national who sells a drug for a rare form of illness into the Republic of Ireland / Northern Ireland. While the sales of the drug were low in USD terms (approx \$100,000 each month), they were extremely lucrative. The US Multi-national sells in

Euros / Sterling and bills once a month, charging at the spot rate available on the day the invoice is issued. This exposes them to currency movements. As these currency movements had been unpredictable in the last number of months, the company had approached John about how best to hedge its exposure.

> **Task 31: Advise Harry as to how best the US Multi-national and IBRT Ltd might manage their respective exposures.**

Patrick calls Harry and is very complimentary on the work you have done for him in relation to the foreign exchange exposures that IRBT faced. He informs Harry that he had presented this to the Board of IRBT the previous week, and that they were becoming much more comfortable with the expansion of the organisation into foreign markets. Harry in turn was delighted from the point of view of Sonner & Saville for two reasons. Firstly as a result of the work you have been doing, IBRT Ltd has expressed a willingness to retain Sonner & Saville for guidance in relation to Foreign Currency transactions. In addition, IBRT Ltd has expressed the need for advice in relation to the management of its other exposures, starting with its interest exposures.

Patrick is due to visit the office of Sonner & Saville tomorrow and has asked Harry for a brief outline of the various considerations involved in managing debt and interest. He has a number of detailed issues that he wants to discuss at the actual meeting but has asked that we first of all prepare the brief. Before you complete tasks 32 to 34 you will need to read up on the Interest Rate Risk section in **Chapter 18** of your text. In addition you should attempt question 6 in the text.

> **Task 32: Prepare a brief memorandum for Patrick describing what is meant by Interest Rate Exposure and the key considerations involved in managing a Debt Portfolio.**

At the meeting Patrick thanked you for the brief and said that it gave him a good introduction to the whole area. He noted that up to this point in time, IBRT Ltd did not manage its interest rate exposure to any great degree, but it had come up at their Board meeting. The Board expressed the view that the rates of interest were about to fall as this seemed to be the general expectation in the financial markets. Therefore, the Board expressed a preference for IBRT Ltd to use variable rate debt. However the Fixed Interest rate available to IBRT Ltd was 6.25% while the variable rate was higher than this at 6.50% (i.e. the current inter bank rate of 4% plus 2.5%). Patrick was in a dilemma. He was not sure how to manage this situation as he did not want to borrow at a higher rate than another that was available, but he did want to have variable rate debt.

You did not say anything during this discussion, as it was not an area with which you were very familiar. However, Harry seemed to know a lot about this and spoke to Patrick about the possibility of using an interest rate swap to help IBRT Ltd achieve its dual desire:

- To have variable debt so it could take advantage of any future downward interest rate movement,
- but at the same time avoid the scenario where it had to pay more for the variable rate debt than the current rate for fixed rate debt.

After the meeting had ended, Harry asked you to remain in the office, and the two of you went on a conference call with Fiona from First Bank PLC. Following a brief discussion where Harry outlines the scenario, Fiona thinks that she may be able to help Patrick out. Basically, a client company of hers (CME Ltd) has been through a few turbulent years as it has tried to move from being a traditional manufacturing company to a software development company. The company has incurred significant annual losses and while their business model looks to be coming through successfully, they do not have as good a credit rating as IBRT Ltd. CME currently has a debt portfolio similar in size to that of IBRT Ltd and they have a preference for fixed rate debt, as they want to have certainty about the cash flows that they will incur in the coming years while their restructuring nears completion. First Bank PLC has offered them variable rate debt at 6.75% and fixed rate debt at 7.25%.

Armed with this information, Harry asks you to outline how IBRT Ltd and CME Ltd might come to a mutually beneficial arrangement to manage their interest rate exposures.

> **Task 33: Outline how IBRT Ltd and CME Ltd might come to a mutually beneficial arrangement to manage their interest rate exposures.**

Patrick is quite pleased when you and Harry share the calculations with him and he feels that this is indeed something that he will be able to take back to the Board. Harry is delighted because the potential saving is another example of the value that the services of Sonner & Saville can bring to the table for their clients. Harry is anxious to emphasise the expertise that Sonner & Saville offer and suggests to Patrick that before the swap is finalised a number of other ways of managing the exposure are looked at. He suggests two such methods, being an interest rate forward agreement and an interest rate option. He asks you to prepare a brief memo for Patrick outlining what each of these entail, and how they might be of benefit to IBRT Ltd in managing its interest rate exposure.

> **Task 34: Prepare a brief memorandum for Patrick describing interest rate forward rate agreements and interest rate options, and how they might be of assistance to IBRT Ltd in managing its exposures.**

During the conversation with Fiona earlier on she happened to mention to Harry the concept of Value at Risk (VAR) which is being used on a more and more frequent basis within the banking sector. Harry asked you to briefly have a look at what this VAR concept entailed and whether or not it might be of any use to Patrick in his current situation.

> **Task 35: Send Harry an e-mail describing Value at Risk and advise as to whether this would be of interest to Patrick.**

SOLUTIONS TO THE TASKS 1–35

Solution to Task 1:

An outline solution is provided only here. Your note should include:

- Financial management and the three elements of which it comprises;
- Financial management's aim is to maximise shareholder wealth;
- Financial strategy which seeks to manage the business's finances in such a way that it supports and is aligned to the business strategy.

Key Stakeholder	Financial objective
Shareholder	Maximise shareholder wealth (dividend and share price), ensure that their investment is not jeopardised through excessive risk taking.
Long term creditors (bankers or debenture holders)	Protecting their position in terms of interest income and protection of capital
Management	Maximise their salaries and bonuses without jeopardising their jobs
Employees	Terms and conditions of employment and job security
Suppliers	Being paid on a timely basis on agreed terms
Customers	Getting goods or services at a reasonable price and on fair credit terms

Solution to Task 2:

	£/€'000
Profit before taxation	1,500
Taxation @ 20%	300
Profit after tax	1,200
Preference dividend (6% * £/€2m)	120
Earnings attributable to ordinary shareholders	1,080
Number of ordinary shares	5m
EPS	21.6 p/c

You note that EPS is based on historic data and profits which we have noted already are open to being manipulated. Shareholders and analysts will be more focused on the future trend and to the extent that the trend is indicative of the future, this is likely to be of interest.

Solution to Task 3:

	Current year	Year 1	Year 2	Year 3	Year 4	Year 5
	€m	€m	€m	€m	€m	€m
Sales	4.00	4.30	5.20	7.40	8.20	9.00
Net profit after tax	0.40	0.43	0.52	0.74	0.82	0.90
Dividends (50% of profits)	0.20	0.22	0.26	0.37	0.41	0.45
Total assets less current liabilities (130% of sales)	5.20	5.59	6.76	9.62	10.66	11.70
Equity (increases by retained earnings)	3.38	3.59	3.85	4.22	4.63	5.08
Maximum debt (35% of long term funds or 53.9% of equity)	1.82	1.93	2.08	2.27	2.50	2.74

| Funds available | 5.20 | 5.52 | 5.93 | 6.49 | 7.13 | 7.82 |
| (Shortfalls) in funds* | 0 | (0.07) | (0.83) | (3.13) | (3.53) | (3.88) |

* Given maximum gearing of 35% and no new issue of shares = funds available less net assets required.

The projections highlight the incompatibility of the various financial targets. Addressing this could be tackled through:

- Raising additional equity from late year 1 onwards;
- Increasing our level of profitability – which in practice may be unrealistic;
- Increasing the asset turnover: the current ratio of 130% appears quite inefficient;
- Reducing our level of dividends – an action that will be unpopular with our shareholders;
- Increasing our level of gearing: this may not be very attractive to our shareholders given the additional financial risk.

Whatever solutions are agreed as noted already, it is critical that the trade-offs and compromises are discussed and agreed at a high level within the organisation.

Solution to Task 4:

Harry

I just wish to bring to your attention that during our meeting I noted that Mr Sahib's brief case was full of cash. He has requested that we lodge money to our own bank account. Having read your briefing on the legal framework I am conscious of the money laundering laws which are now in place and am concerned that we might inadvertently breach these.

Regards

James

Solution to Task 5:

To: harryoneill@sonner&saville.com

From: Jamescrown@sonner&saville.com

Re: Advantages and disadvantages for IBRT Ltd of having a stock exchange quotation

Harry,

I have outlined below the main advantages and disadvantages for IBRT Ltd of having a Stock Market quotation

Regards,

James

Advantages

- Flotation increases the access that a company will have to equity capital, not just at the initial launch stage but also at future stages of the company's evolvement. If a company is not publicly quoted it can be harder to raise equity finance as there is not a ready market for its shares.
- Liquidity is increased for equity shareholders, and it becomes easier to buy and sell shares as there is a ready market available on a daily basis. This is much more cumbersome in a private company.
- A quotation puts a value on the company based on its current market value.
- If a company raises finance through the issue of equity, payment of a dividend is not compulsory. With debt there is an obligation to pay back both the interest and capital elements.
- A quotation enhances the public profile and credibility of the quoted company. This increases awareness not just in the general marketplace, but also with its customers and suppliers. It assures them that the company's governance processes are of a high standard.
- Having a stock market quotation allows the company to come up with more imaginative ways to reward their employees. It can help create employee loyalty through share purchase discount and share option schemes.
- The company can use equity as consideration as part of a takeover strategy.

Disadvantages

- There can be control implications when shares in the company are issued, as new investors come into the organisation. Also, management decision-making will be subject to much closer scrutiny.
- The costs associated with an issue can be very high. Such costs encompass legal fees, underwriting costs, accounting costs, issue house costs, advertising costs etc.
- There is an increased regulatory burden placed upon the company due to its listing on the stock exchange. This includes an increased onus on directors in terms of their dealings as well as extensive corporate governance and reporting requirements. In addition, the type of information that has to be disclosed can become quite intrusive, especially where an organisation was used to dealing with issues in-house.
- Once quoted on the market, the value of the company may vary not just due to company specific issues, but also due to the prevailing sentiment on the market. This is called market risk exposure.
- There may be a significant tie up of management time at the time of issue. This may detract from the successful working of the company.

Solution to Task 6:

To: Harry O'Neill

From: James Crown

Re: Stock Exchange requirements

Harry,

I have outlined below a brief summary of the various exchanges open to IBRT Ltd, the main initial listing requirements, as well as the main ongoing reporting requirements. I have prepared as detailed a brief as possible in the time available to me, but if you need more detail please do not hesitate to come back to me,

Regards,

James

(i) Various Exchanges open to IBRT Ltd

- In the Republic of Ireland there is the Irish Stock Exchange which is broken into two markets, the official list (being large companies and government bonds) and the IEX (small to medium sized companies).
- In the UK the main exchange is the London Stock Exchange and this is made up of two key markets for equity shares; The Main market and the Alternative Investments market (The AIM). Another option is the PLUS market which has a primary exchange and a secondary exchange for small and mid-size companies.

(ii) Initial Listing requirements

The main requirements that would need to be fulfilled by IBRT Ltd to gain an initial listing on the main stock exchange in the Republic of Ireland are as follows;

(i) Market capitalisation

The expected aggregate market value of all securities to be listed must be at least:

- €1 million for shares; and
- €200,000 for debt securities

(ii) Accounts

A new applicant must have published or filed audited accounts that:

- cover at least three years;
- are the latest accounts for a period ended not more than 6 months before the date of the prospectus;
- have been reported on by the auditors without modification.

(iii) Shares in public hands

- 25% of shares must, no later than the time of admission, be distributed to the public
- A percentage lower than 25% may be acceptable to the ISE if the market will operate properly with a lower percentage in view of the large number of shares of the same class and the extent of their distribution to the public.

The main requirements that would need to be fulfilled by IBRT Ltd gain an initial listing on the main stock exchange in London are as follows;

LR 2 – Requirements for Listing

(i) Market capitalisation

The expected aggregate market value of all securities to be listed must be at least:

- £700,000 for shares, and
- £200,000 for debt securities

LR 6 – Additional requirements for listing for equity securities

(i) Accounts

A new applicant must have published or filed audited accounts that:

- cover at least three years
- are the latest accounts for a period ended not more than 6 months before the date of the prospectus or listing particulars
- have been reported on by the auditors without modification

(ii) Shares in public hands

- 25% of shares must, no later than the time of admission, be distributed to the public.
- A percentage lower than 25% may be acceptable to the Financial Services Authority if the market will operate properly with a lower percentage in view of the large number of shares of the same class and the extent of their distribution to the public.

(iii) Ongoing Reporting Requirements

In order to ensure ongoing adequacy of information for the market, the Stock Exchange imposes a set of continuing obligations on quoted companies which must be complied with. The main aim of these continuing obligations is to ensure that price sensitive information is released to the market without delay. This is extremely important if the investing community is to have confidence in the operation of the market, and it minimises the risk of one party buying or selling shares with the benefit of information which is unavailable to another party involved in the transaction.

Some of the main occasions on which public announcements must be made include **inter alia:-**

- A change in the financial condition of a company which would have a material effect on its share price.
- Major changes or developments in a company's activities, such as new products, contracts or customers.
- The preliminary announcements of profits for the year *(finals)* or half year *(interims)*.
- A decision to pay or not to pay a dividend.
- Details of an acquisition or realisation of assets.
- Changes in the interests of directors and persons connected with them in the company's shares.
- A change in directors or in the functions or executive responsibilities of a director.
- Notification to the company by shareholders whose holding exceeds or falls below 3% of the company's issued shares carrying voting rights or moves through another whole percentage point above 3%.

While this is not an exhaustive list it does go some way to identifying the ongoing reporting requirements for a quoted company.

Solution to Task 7:

To: harryoneill@sonner&saville.com

From: Jamescrown@sonner&saville.com

Re: Types of share issues available to IBRT Ltd & associated issues

Harry,

I have set out below the main ways in which shares in a company can be issued as part of obtaining a Stock Market flotation.

(i) Offer for Sale by Prospectus

This is the most expensive way of issuing shares and is generally only done for the very largest of share issues. A company will require the services of a sponsoring company / issuing house who will manage the share issue for the company, a brokering agency, accountants, solicitors, advertisers etc.

Therefore it is quite likely that the cost would be prohibitive unless the issue is a major one.

(ii) Offer for Sale by subscription

This is similar to an offer for sale by prospectus, but the whole issue is not underwritten as the company may experience difficulty in doing so. If there is not sufficient public demand the company may decide to cancel the entire issue.

(iii) Issue by tender

This can be useful where there is genuine difficulty in determining the price of a share that is being launched on the market. Here the issue price is not fixed, unlike a prospectus issue. Members of the public are invited to tender for the shares at prices they feel are warranted. When the tenders are received an issue price is then determined based on the supply and demand. Any tender above the issue price will receive the shares tendered for (and receive back any surplus monies tendered). Any below will not.

(iv) A Placing

A situation where the sponsor arranges for most of the issue to be bought by a small number of investors (usually institutional investors such as pension funds and insurance companies) is called a placing. The Stock Exchange will usually insist on several institutional investors being involved in this to ensure the marketability of the shares when they are launched on the market. This is much cheaper and less risky than a prospectus issue although fewer shares will trade openly on the market, as there will be less investors with shares to sell.

(v) Intermediaries offer

This is the same as a placing except that the issuing company does not employ an issuing house to arrange the placement, but does so itself by identifying interested investors or brokers. This can result in less liquidity for the shares than with a placing.

(vi) Vendor Placing

This occurs where there is a takeover. Company A may wish to takeover Company B and wants to do so by issuing new shares in Company A as consideration. However the shareholders in Company B want to receive cash as their consideration for the takeover and not shares. Hence Company A will issue enough new shares to the market that will allow it to raise the necessary funds to pay cash to the shareholders in Company B.

(vii) Stock Exchange Introduction

Here no shares are made available to the market but the Stock Exchange still grants a quotation. This will only occur where there are a large number of shareholders in the company already. The main reason for the quotation is to improve the marketability of the shares. This can be quite cheap as there are no underwriting or issue costs.

Other Considerations

- Regardless of the method being used to issue the shares, one of the most critical factors that IBRT Ltd would have to take advice on is the issue price. If this is set too low then the issue will damage the wealth of the existing shareholders, as they will be giving away some of the value of the company. On the other hand if it is set too high they run the risk of the issue not being fully subscribed and not raising all the funds required.
- One way for IBRT Ltd to minimise the risk that not all the shares will be taken up is to have the issue underwritten. This is where an Issuing House or sponsoring company guarantees to buy any remaining unallocated shares at a certain price following the issue. This means that IBRT Ltd would effectively have a base price on any issue of shares.
- Timing is another critical issue. The market can suffer from huge volatility at times. Trying to catch the market in an upward curve or at a time when sentiment is favourable can be extremely difficult. This is where the advice from any brokers that IBRT Ltd employ would be critical.

Solution to Task 8:

To: Harry O'Neill

From: James Crown

Re: Considerations in formulating a dividend policy

Harry,

The purpose of dividend policy in an organisation is to maximise shareholder wealth.

In formulating a dividend policy, there are a number of considerations which will always need to be taken into account by a company. I have detailed these below but if you need further information please do not hesitate to call me.

Regards,

James

Dividends have an important role to play in the valuation of an organisation. One way investors value a company is by using the Dividend Valuation model. This model gives a significant weighting in the overall valuation of a company to the dividends that a company pays. The model attaches importance not just to the actual dividend but also the rate of growth in the dividend. Therefore IBRT Ltd also needs to look at the growth factor and what signal that gives to the shareholder. While Modigliani & Miller questioned the relevance of Dividends in valuing an organisation, their postulation was later discounted as it ignored the effect of taxation, risk preferences of investors and transaction costs.

Some practical considerations in relation to dividends

- A company must have enough **liquid funds** to actually pay the dividend that they are about to declare. As profitability and cash are not one and the same thing, it does not always follow that an organisation can pay all of its dividends in cash.

- IBRT Ltd will need to be **profitable** in the long run in order to pay dividends. While a company can make short term losses and still have the cash resources to pay out previously declared dividends, this is a situation that can only carry on for so long. To be fair this does not appear to be an issue for IBRT Ltd as it has been profitable for the last five years and has retained approximately 70% of its profits in the company each year.
- Does the company need to retain earnings to finance **new activities** or can the finance be readily obtained elsewhere? In the case of IBRT Ltd, if it lets a payment of €/£10M go to shareholders in the form of dividend, is there some financing requirement over the horizon where IBRT Ltd will need to raise that €/£10M again? If they feel they will not be able to do so, then maybe they should question the wisdom of making the dividend payment now.
- There are **legislative provisions** in the various Companies Acts and Orders that limit the amount of dividend a limited company can pay out to a maximum of its accumulated realised profits less its accumulated realised losses. This is further tightened for PLCs by taking unrealised losses into account.
- **Inflation** can be an issue that influences dividend policy as the company needs to maintain cash and profits within the company to ensure that they have the same operating capacity as in a prior year.
- There may be **restrictive clauses** contained in long term debt issues by the company which restrict the amount of profit that can be distributed by the company. In addition, the Articles and Memorandum of Association of the company may also impose limits on what dividends can be distributed. Patrick will need to review any such documents he believes are relevant, to ascertain if this is an issue.
- The **taxation profile** of the shareholders in the company will have a big bearing on the attractiveness of dividends for investors. Dividends are subject to income tax rates. The gain on a sale of shares is subject to capital gains tax. An individual shareholder may have a preference for one over the other depending on their individual taxation situation. Patrick may need to consider the make up of IBRT Ltd's shareholder base before coming to any conclusions on this issue.
- Dividends are often regarded as a **signal** to investors about the prospects of a company in the future. Any change in dividend policy may be viewed as a change in the way that management feel about the future prospects for the organisation. In general investors will usually expect a

consistent dividend policy from the company with stable dividends or better still, steady dividend growth as this sends out a powerful message about the company's prospects.

There are two approaches to interpreting the dividend payouts. The first says that a high dividend leads to an increase in a company's value as it signals to the market that a company can afford to pay out a high rate of dividend in the future. It postulates that shareholders have a preference for dividends over capital gain (maybe for taxation reasons, a preference for cash in the hand or due to fees associated with the buying and selling of shares).

The other approach takes the view that a lower level of dividend leads to an increase in a company's value. Such reasoning identifies shareholders with a preference for capital gain via share price growth, rather than dividend income. It also sees the retention of earnings in the company as a signal that the company has a number of excellent opportunities available in which to invest.

Patrick will need to look at the clientele of shareholders in IBRT Ltd to see which is the best approach to formulating dividend policy.

Solution to Task 9:

To: Patrickmurphy@ibrt.com

Cc: harryoneill@sonner&saville.com

From: Jamescrown@sonner&saville.com

Re: The types of distributions that can be made by IBRT Ltd

Patrick,

I have provided below a brief synopsis of some of the other types of distributions available to IBRT Ltd. Harry is on vacation for a few days but if you are unclear on any of the detail below please do not hesitate to call me.

(i) Stock Splits:

Here, the number of shares in a company are increased in a set proportion (e.g. in a 'two for one split' two new shares are issued for each existing share). This is not really a distribution as it just changes the number of shares in the company. It can however be beneficial in a company where individual shares have a very high price, as a stock split makes them more marketable and liquid, and hence more attractive to purchase or sell.

(ii) A Scrip dividend

This is a dividend payment which takes the form of new shares instead of cash. This has the effect of providing a dividend but does not involve the company paying out cash.

(iii) A Bonus or Scrip issue

This involves the issue of new shares to existing shareholders in proportion to their existing holdings. The main benefit here is to make the shares in a company more marketable.

(iv) Share Repurchase

Under legislation, a company can repurchase its own shares either by buying them back in the stock market, making an offer to all equity shareholders, or by approaching individual equity shareholders. This can be attractive for a company that has spare cash as it helps reduce the share base for future EPS calculations. If left idle the shareholders may penalise the company for not making better use of their cash resources. In addition, if the company feels that the market is undervaluing their shares, they may perceive this as a good time to buy back some of those undervalued shares. Finally, share repurchase schemes can be aimed at unwelcome or dissatisfied shareholders to ease their burden on the company.

Best wishes,

James

Solution to Task 10:

There can be any number of reasons why organisations engage in Merger and Acquisition activity. The most common are listed below with a brief comment on each:

(i) **Synergy:** One would expect that when two organisations join together they do so in the expectation that the sum will be greater than the individual parts that make up the new entity. Quite often synergistic benefits are perceived to be in the area of costs, where maybe one organisation has unused capacity or a lower cost base than another entity, and can increase profitability by realigning the overall organisation's cost base to that of the lower cost base entity. However there can also be other synergies in terms of increased access to lower cost of capital and increased size in a market leading to more revenue. In general it helps to think of synergistic benefits in terms of increased economies of scale. Basically the synergistic benefits of an Acquisition or Merger should be such that the value of the combined organisation is greater than the value of the stand alone entities.

(ii) **Access to a skill base or management team.** Quite often an organisation will look to merge or takeover another not because of a particular product or service, but because there exists within the target organisation a particular skill set that might be very expensive to build up internally or may take too long to do so. This skill set could be in a technical area of expertise or in the ability of management to drive performance. Whatever the rationale, the purchase of the skill set is paramount.

(iii) **Diversification** can be another motive for Merger and Acquisition activity. Once an organisation perceives that it needs to diversify into another industry or market, the quickest way can well be through an acquisition or a merger. Organisations diversify to spread their risk away from over reliance on one industry or product offering, and to ensure the best long term return for the shareholders in the company. There is of course a counter argument which says that there is no need for any company to diversify on behalf of their shareholder base, as these shareholders are quite free to diversify on their own behalf if they so wish.

(iv) **Growth.** A company may look at the cost and timescale associated with growing through its internal operations and may deem this to be too slow or expensive a process. When this occurs, takeovers and mergers (ie growth by acquisition) are often considered as the best route.

(v) **The improvement of Financial Risk.** A company with risky earnings may consider acquiring or merging with a company that has more steady earnings to reduce the overall risk associated with their

72 STRATEGIC FINANCE AND MANAGEMENT ACCOUNTING TOOLKIT

company. Similarly, companies may seek to take over other entities that have a more solid asset base or liquidity situation than their own, so that they reduce their overall risk.

(vi) **Undervalued assets**. If an organisation feels that the value of another company is understated vis-à-vis its assets or its income, they may wish to acquire that company and realise the true value of those assets and earnings. This will add to the overall value of the shareholders of the acquiring company.

(vii) **Management Motives.** Mergers and Acquisitions may not be motivated purely by the best interest of the ordinary shareholders in the company, but may have more to do with the personal motivations of individual managers. In general these reasons relate to areas such as prestige, executive compensation, power growth and empire creation. These can supplant the traditionally accepted motive of maximising the value of an organisation to the ordinary shareholders.

(viii) While most of the above reasons for acquisitions and mergers are viewed from the point of view of the acquiring company, quite often the reason for the merger or takeover can be that **the target may wish to sell part of all of their operation.** This can be due to the fact that some of the shareholders want to get out of the organisation and realise their value in the company. Others may want to bring new skill sets on board that will allow the company to grow and compete into the future as part of a new merged entity.

Solution to Task 11:

To: harryoneill@sonner&saville.com

From: Jamescrown@sonner&saville.com

Re: Bullet points for due diligence call

Harry,

As requested I have outlined below a list of the areas that I believe Jones Bros Ltd would consider looking at in the course of a normal due diligence. I developed the list from my own research, as well as speaking to John Keane as suggested.

(i) Sales,

(ii) Purchases,

(iii) Operating activities,

(iv) Property,

(v) Legal matters

(vi) Pensions.

(vii) Trademarks, patents and other intellectual property

(viii) Can they integrate the company into their organisation in the most tax efficient manner possible?

(ix) Are there related party transactions included in the historical earnings that were conducted under pricing arrangements that do not reflect true cost?

(x) Employee skill sets

(xi) Outstanding contracts

(xii) Key customer satisfaction

(xiii) Exposures

(xiv) Financing

(xv) Investment opportunities

(xvi) Audited accounts

(xvii) Internal Management Accounts

(xviii) Are historical earnings sustainable?

(xix) Are forecasts based on reasonable assumptions?

(xx) Are assets correctly valued?

(xxi) Are there off balance sheet liabilities that are relevant?

While this list is not exhaustive, it does at least give you some guidance as to how the call later on might develop. I will continue to look at this list and identify any further areas that might be relevant.

Regards,

James

Solution to Task 12:

Following discussion with Harry it is decided that you will use four methods of valuation in order to put a potential value on the company. These are:

- The Net Assets based valuation method
- Earnings based valuation
- Capitalised earnings Approach
- Dividend based valuation method

(i) Net Assets Based Valuation:

	€/£ M's
Value of Net Assets @ 31 December 2008	139
Increase in value of 'Other Investments' figure (Note 1)	35
Increase in value of buildings	70
Increase in value of Debentures	(5)
Decrease in value of Debtors	(4)
Goodwill	(20)
Adjusted Net Asset Value of IBRT Ltd	215
Number of Shares in issue	20 Million
Value per share	€/£10.75

Note 1: Assumes current value of €/£65M being the mid-point between the rejected offer and the expected value upon flotation.

The main issue with the use of an asset Based Valuation method is that this is a valuation of an organisation based on a 'worst case' scenario. It takes the view that the company does not continue to trade and drive earnings in the future, and instead is broken up, the assets sold and the liabilities paid off. In reality, this is unlikely to occur unless the company is being bought as part of a break-up or asset stripping exercise. As a result, the asset based valuation will tend to place a floor price on any bidding war that might ensue in relation to a merger or takeover.

(ii) Earnings Based Valuation

Step 1: Calculate maintainable Earnings after taxation

	€/£ M's	€/£ M's
Profit after taxation – year ended		
31 December 2008		35
Add: Rationalisation Benefits	10	
Operational Savings (After Tax)	7	17
		52
Less: Closure of Division – Loss of profits		(4)
Maintainable Earnings		48

Step 2: Calculate the P/E ratio

As the two quoted companies are similar to IBRT Ltd and are quoted on the stock exchange, a Mid-point P/E ratio would be 10. Allowing a 20% discount for the fact that IBRT Ltd is unquoted would suggest a P/E ratio of 8.

Step 3: Calculate the value of IBRT Ltd

	€/£ M's	€/£ M's
Value of IBRT Ltd (P/E ratio ×		
Maintainable earnings)		384
Less: Cost of achieving increase in profits		
Rationalisation Plan costs	(50)	
Redundancy costs	(3)	(53)
		331
Number of Shares		20 Million
Value per share		€/£16.55

The main issue in calculating the value of a company in this way is that the calculation is dependent on the validity of two pieces of information (i.e., the P/E ratio and an earnings figure). There are issues associated with the use of either piece of information.

In relation to the P/E ratio the following issues apply;

- The P/E ratio is based on historical data, while we are trying to put a value on a company based on what will occur in the future.

- If we are trying to derive a P/E ratio from comparative quoted companies, this raises the question as to how comparable those organisations really are with our own. While they may look similar or operate in similar industries, each organisation is unique.
- Typically if we do come up with a P/E ratio that we are comfortable with, we may still need to make arbitrary adjustments because of other factors. These include things such as industry trends in terms of growth or stagnation, general economic and financial conditions, financial risk associated with the new company, the degree of asset backing or liquidity of a company, the amount of key knowledge invested in a few people in the company etc. Therefore, the P/E ratio finally settled on to value a company may be arbitrary. The seller will obviously be trying to push this up while the buyer will be trying to understate it, as it will have a major impact on the valuation of an organisation.

In relation to the Earnings figure the following issues are relevant;

- The figure for maintainable earnings is the profit figure for the latest financial year, plus or minus any profits or losses that will not appear in future years. The seller will be motivated to classify any losses as relating to the past year only. The buyer will be trying to ring fence some element of the profit as unique to the past year and hence not maintainable going forward.
- If there is an element of earnings growth forecasted into the figure for maintainable earnings going forward, then this is again a figure that will be subject for discussion and negotiation. All such forecasts should be reasonable and made in good faith.
- A company's choice of accounting policies would need to be clearly understood by any potential valuer.

Therefore it can be seen that any estimate of maintainable earnings and P/E ratios is merely that: an estimate. Consequently, a process of negotiation would ensue in any potential merger or acquisition activity.

(iii) The Capitalised Earnings approach

In theory the optimal way to value a company is to estimate all the future cash inflows and outflows associated with the company and discount these to present values. In reality this is very difficult to do as there would be a lot of uncertainty in identifying what the future cash flows associated with an organisation might be, and it would be difficult to estimate what the effect of the merger or takeover would be on those cash flows.

The capitalised earnings approach is a proxy for this approach as it starts with the maintainable earnings figure calculated above and effectively treats this as the best estimate of future cash flows.

The method assumes that maintainable earnings are effectively an annual cash flow in perpetuity. To get the Present Value of a cash flow in perpetuity, one divides the annual cash flow by the rate of return that the company requires. This yields the present value of the future cash flows. One then subtracts any costs to be incurred upfront to create this cash flow in perpetuity, and you are left with the present value of the equity share capital.

	€/£ M's	€/£ M's
Maintainable earnings		48
Yield required by Jones Bros Ltd		18%
Present value of Future cash flows		267
Less: Cost of achieving increase in profits		
Rationalisation Plan costs	(50)	
Redundancy costs	(3)	
		(53)
		214
Number of Shares		20 Million
Value per share		€/£10.70

There are a number of drawbacks to this valuation method, the main ones being the difficulty in forecasting future trading results, the difficulty in establishing a cost of capital that will take into account the effect of the acquisition on the future costs of raising additional capital, and the difficulty in forecasting the synergistic gains from a possible merger.

(iv) Dividend Valuation Model

This method of valuation is normally used in valuing a minority stake. The use of a valuation method focusing on Dividends is very much taking the view that the shareholding in the company is spread in such a way that a shareholder cannot, in normal circumstances, influence the level of earnings retained in the company. Therefore their primary concern will be with the level of dividends receivable. Therefore, it is the dividend that gives value to the company from their perspective.

In the case of IBRT Ltd, the dividend growth model can be used to try and put a value on the shares in IBRT Ltd. This maintains that we can value a company using the following formula:

$$MV = \frac{Do\ (1 + g)}{(r - g)}$$ Where Do = the most recent Dividend
g = the growth rate of the company's dividend
r = the shareholder's required rate of return

We know from the information provided that the most recent dividend is likely to be €/£10M. In addition, we were told earlier when engaged in calculating that figure, that the shareholders in Jones Bros required rate of return is 18%. We need to calculate the rate of dividend growth.

We take the dividend in 2008 which is proposed to be €/£10M and that in 2004 which was €/£6M. The dividend has grown by a factor of 1.67 (i.e. €/£10M / €/£6M) in this period. This represents four growth periods. By calculating the cube root of 1.67 we will be able to get the average growth rate for the period. The cube root is 1.137 so the average growth rate is 13.7%

Inserting this into our formula above we get the following outcome

MV	=	Do $(1 + g)$ / $(r - g)$
MV	=	€/£10M (1.137) / (0.18 − 0.137)
MV	=	€/£11.37M / 0.043
MV	=	€/£264.40M
Number of Shares		20 Million
Value per share		€ / £13.22

The main drawback of this method of share valuation is that it is very much focused on a minority shareholding. This is not the case in valuing IBRT Ltd, as, were Jones Bros to go ahead and attempt to buy the company, they would be acquiring a majority shareholding. In addition, calculating a cost of capital may be a complex operation for a company that is not quoted.

Summary

Method of Valuation	Total value (M's)	Value per Share
Net Assets	€/£215	€/£10.75
Earnings Based	€/£331	€/£16.55
Capitalised Earnings	€/£214	€/£10.70
Dividend Based	€/£264	€/£13.22

The four prices calculated above are really just starting points in terms of producing a valuation of IBRT Ltd, but at least it will help to identify a range of values on which discussion may centre.

Solution to Task 13:

To: Harry O'Neill

From: James Crown

Re: Possible Anti-takeover measures available to Mary Patterson

Harry,

While there are a number of avenues open to Mary in terms of resisting any potential offer from Jones Bros Ltd, I have detailed below the most common ones used. It will of course need to be considered that any action taken must be in the interests of the shareholders of IBRT Ltd.

(i) **Shark Repellents:** These are unpleasant things designed to trigger should a takeover go ahead. These make the target company quite unattractive to potential suitors. In Mary's case these could involve drawing up some agreements, say with banks, to make their loans instantly repayable upon takeover, passing a provision requiring a 100% approval for a takeover etc.

(ii) **Golden Parachutes:** Mary can ensure that generous payments are arranged for her and / or whoever she wishes should any takeover go ahead. This will make any takeover less attractive for Jones Bros Ltd.

(iii) **Poison Pills:** These are best described as actions that would amount to economic suicide should a bid go ahead. Mary could look at some of IBRT Ltd's more lucrative contracts for example and agree that they will pull out of those contracts should control of the company change.

(iv) **The Crown Jewels Lockup:** IBRT Ltd might threaten to sell off some of their more valuable assets in the event of any takeover bid going ahead. If Mary was to try to use this method of defence, she will need to have a very good understanding of exactly why IBRT Ltd is attractive to Jones Bros Ltd, and what assets they value within the organisation. In addition, she will have to find a willing buyer for those assets, who is willing to leave an open offer while the takeover discussions are ongoing.

(v) **A White Knight:** This could involve Mary seeking a friendly company to compete in the bidding for IBRT Ltd. If Mary does not want to sell at all, this may not be a useful defence, but if she is forced to sell, this could work for her and may also drive up the price of the company

(vi) **A White Squire Defence:** Here Mary would effectively place shares in the hands of a friendly party, who would have no interest in taking control of IBRT Ltd, but would have enough of a holding to make any bid by Jones Bros Ltd unattractive.

(vii) **The Pacman Defence:** This would involve IBRT Ltd making a hostile bid for Jones Bros Ltd. In this instance it would be hard to see something like this working for Mary, as she would need to have the whole Board in favour of this action and the likelihood of being able to come to an arrangement with the shareholders of Jones Bros Ltd might be improbable.

(ix) **A Standstill Agreement:** Here, Mary would reach an agreement with Jones Bros Ltd that they would not expand their shareholding beyond a certain percentage for a specified period of time.

(x) Launch a **defensive advertising campaign:** As the number of shareholders in IBRT Ltd is small this may not be as effective as Mary would like, and perhaps personal approaches might be more satisfactory.

(xi) **Litigation:** This can be used by Mary as a delaying tactic, and in the context of EU legislation around monopolies and mergers it can be quite effective. A lot will depend on how unique the offering of the new merged entity would be in the market place.

Regards,

James

Solution to Task 14:

To: Mary Patterson

Cc: Harry O'Neill

From: James Crown

Re: Financial performance of Giles Ltd over the last number of years

Mary,

You have asked me to look at the financial performance of Giles Ltd over the last number of years. It is worth noting at this point that the information you have provided is not enough to form an overall picture of the company's performance in the last number of years. In order to do this I would need to have access to the profit and loss information.

However, notwithstanding this, I have performed a partial analysis based on the information provided.

(i) Calculation of two key ratios

- Current Ratio $=$ $\dfrac{\text{Current Assets}}{\text{Current Liabilities}}$

	31.12.07 Actual €/£M's	31.12.08 Actual €/£M's	31.03.09 Projected €/£M's
$=$	$\dfrac{700}{260}$ $=$	$\dfrac{1,060}{800}$ $=$	$\dfrac{1,170}{1,070}$
$=$	2.70 $=$	1.32 $=$	1.09

- Debt / Equity ratio $= \dfrac{\text{Debentures/Loans/Overdraft}}{\text{Ord Shares/Pref shares/Reserves}}$

	31.12.07 Actual €/£M's	31.12.08 Actual €/£M's	31.03.09 Projected €/£M's
$=$	$\dfrac{100}{990}$ $=$	$\dfrac{600}{750}$ $=$	$\dfrac{790}{710}$
$=$	0.10 $=$	0.80 $=$	1.11

(ii) Analysis of key ratios

- **Gearing:** As can be seen from the above analysis, Giles Ltd has been funding its activities in the last number of years by accessing debt capital. This has seen the company's debt rise from €/£100M on the 31/12/07 to €/£790M in the space of 15 months. Furthermore, €/£570M of this debt is in the form of a bank overdraft. A bank overdraft is technically repayable on demand, so the financial risk of the company has increased hugely in the last 15 months. The net result of this from a financing perspective, is that the company has gone from a position of debt being approximately 10% of funding, to making up over 50% of funding.

  The company has placed a significant burden on itself in terms of the maturity of the debt that it has taken on itself. Of the total debt of €/£790M, approximately 72% is short-term debt. Also the debenture stock of €/£100M is due to be repaid in 2010.

- **Investment:** The company's inventory levels have been building up quite significantly in the last 15 months, rising almost 70% between the 31/12/07 and the 31/3/09. This is reflective of the trouble that the company has been experiencing in off-loading their properties in the current economic climate. In addition, the company has been making quite a substantial investment in plant and machinery. As a result of this investment activity the required level of funding for the company has also risen, and it is for this purpose that the extra debt being taken on is being used.

- **Liquidity:** The company's liquidity situation has also worsened dramatically in the last 15 months from a healthy Current Ratio of 2.70 on 31/12/07 to a much tighter one of 1.09 by 31/3/09. If we consider that the bulk of current assets at 31/03/09 is made up of inventory, then this is clearly a much worse position to be in. In fact the quick ratio (a comparison of current assets less inventory compared to current Liabilities) is down at 0.065 and is a very good indicator of the liquidity issues facing the company. Were the creditors or the banks to seek to have their monies repaid, the company would probably not be able to convert their inventory into cash in time to pay them and avert liquidation proceedings.

All in all the balance sheet indicates a company that has been building up excess inventory and investing in new plant and machinery in an environment when housing stock is getting harder to move. In addition, it is funding these increased investments exclusively from debt capital, and short-term debt capital at that.

As noted in the introduction, I would need to get some information in relation to the Income Statement in order to complete my analysis.

Solution to Task 15:

To: Mary Patterson

Cc: Harry O'Neill

From: James Crown

Re: Financial performance of Giles Ltd over the last number of years

Mary,

Thank you for the additional Profit & Loss account information that you have provided me with. I have now amended my original memorandum in relation to Giles Ltd. While it does not improve the picture, it does help to provide a more complete view of the organisation and how it has been performing.

(i) Calculation of key ratios

- **Current Ratio** $\quad = \quad \dfrac{\text{Current Assets}}{\text{Current Liabilities}}$

	31.12.07 Actual €/£M's		31.12.08 Actual €/£M's		31.03.09 Projected €/£M's
=	$\dfrac{700}{260}$	=	$\dfrac{1,060}{800}$	=	$\dfrac{1,170}{1,070}$
=	2.70	=	1.32	=	1.09

- **Debt / Equity ratio** $\quad = \quad \dfrac{\text{Debentures / Loans / Overdraft}}{\text{Ord Shares / Pref shares/Reserves}}$

	31.12.07 Actual €/£M's		31.12.08 Actual €/£M's		31.03.09 Projected €/£M's
=	$\dfrac{100}{990}$	=	$\dfrac{600}{750}$	=	$\dfrac{790}{710}$
=	0.10	=	0.80	=	1.11

- **Gross Margin** $\quad = \quad \dfrac{\text{Gross profit} \times 100}{\text{Sales}}$

	Year ended 31.12.07 Actual €/£M's		Year ended 31.12.08 Actual €/£M's		3 Mths ended 31.03.09 Projected €/£M's
=	$\dfrac{340}{2,000}$	=	$\dfrac{100}{1,700}$	=	$\dfrac{60}{350}$
=	17%	=	6%	=	17%

- **Net Margin** $=$ $$\frac{\text{Net Profit / (Loss)} \times 100}{\text{Sales}}$$

	Year ended 31.12.07 Actual €/£M's	Year ended 31.12.08 Actual €/£M's	3 Mths ended 31.03.09 Projected €/£M's
$=$	$\dfrac{20}{2000}$ $=$	$\dfrac{(240)}{1700}$ $=$	$\dfrac{(40)}{350}$
$=$	1% $=$	(14%) $=$	(11%)

- **Interest as a percentage of sales** $=$ $$\frac{\text{Interest Expense} \times 100}{\text{Sales}}$$

	Year ended 31.12.07 Actual €/£M's	Year ended 31.12.08 Actual €/£M's	3 Mths ended 31.03.09 Projected €/£M's
$=$	$\dfrac{0}{2{,}000}$ $=$	$\dfrac{(120)}{1{,}700}$ $=$	$\dfrac{(50)}{350}$
$=$	0% $=$	(7%) $=$	(14%)

(ii) Analysis of key ratios

- **Gearing:** As can be seen from the above analysis, Giles Ltd has been funding its activities in the last number of years by accessing debt capital. This has seen the company's debt rise from €/£100M on the 31/12/07 to €/£790M in the space of 15 months. Furthermore, €/£570M of this debt is in the form of a bank overdraft. A bank overdraft is technically repayable on demand so the financial risk of the company has increased hugely in the last 15 months. The net result of this from a financing perspective, is that the company has gone from a position of debt being approximately 10% of funding, to making up over 50% of funding.

The company has placed a significant burden on itself in terms of the maturity of the debt that it has taken on itself. Of the total debt of €/£790M, approximately 72% is short-term debt. Also the debenture stock of €/£100M is due to be repaid in 2010.

- **Interest Cover:** There has been a major impact on the Income Statement as a result of the nature of the funding. Basically, interest costs as a percentage of sales have risen from zero in 2007 to 14% of sales in the three months ending 31/03/09. Thus, the company's capital structure is having an increasingly adverse impact on the profitability of the company.

- **Investment:** The company's inventory levels have also been building up quite significantly in the last 15 months, rising almost 70% between the 31/12/07 and the 31/3/09. This is reflective of the trouble that the company has been experiencing in off-loading their properties in the current economic climate. In addition, the company has been making quite a substantial investment in plant and machinery. As a result of this investment activity, the required level of funding for the company has also risen, and it is for this purpose that the extra debt being taken on is being used.

- **Profitability:** In terms of profitability, the company had a very poor year in the 12 months ended 31/12/08 mainly due to a drop in the gross margin. Presumably this was as a result of having to drop selling prices due to having an excess stock of houses on hand. However, this appears to be more favourable in the last three months with gross margins getting back up to their 2007 levels, net margins improving over 2008 (though still negative, in the main due to the increase in interest payments).

- **Liquidity:** The company's liquidity situation has also worsened dramatically in the last 15 months from a healthy Current Ratio of 2.70 on 31/12/07 to a much tighter one of 1.09 by 31/3/09. If we consider that the bulk of current assets at 31/03/09 is made up of inventory then this is clearly a much worse position to be in. In fact the quick ratio (a comparison of current assets less inventory compared to current liabilities) is down at 0.065 and this is a very good indicator of the liquidity issues facing the company. Were the creditors or the banks to seek to have their monies repaid, the company would probably not be able to convert their inventory into cash in time to pay them and avert liquidation proceedings.

All in all the balance sheets indicate a company that has been building up excess inventory and investing in new plant & machinery in an environment when housing stock is getting harder to move. In addition, it is funding these increased investments exclusively from debt capital, and short-term debt capital at that. The Profit and loss Account, while showing a more favourable gross margin in the first three months of 2009 was severely affected by the slowdown in housing sales in 2008 and by the interest payments associated with the debt in 2008 and 2009.

Solution to Task 16:

The following is the cash position should the company cease to trade from the 31/03/09;

Break-up value of assets as at 31/03/09	€/£ M's
Land & Buildings	550
Plant & Machinery	70
Value of Inventory	600
Value of Debtors	30
	1,250

Total Liabilities at 31/03/09	€/£M's
10% Secured Debt	100
Other Secured Loans	120
Bank Overdraft	570
Trade Creditors	500
	1,290

From the above analysis it can be seen that if Giles Ltd was forced into liquidation, while the 10% Debenture holders and the other secured loans would get paid in full, there would be only €/£1,030M remaining to pay the bank Overdraft and the Trade creditors. In addition, if we took the liquidation costs of €/£100M into account, that would leave only €/£930M or €/£0.87c for every Euro/Pound owed.

There would be no residual monies for either the Ordinary or preference Shareholders.

Solution to Task 17:

In order to ascertain the future funding requirements for Giles Ltd, it is necessary to look at the cash flow forecasts for the next number of years.

Basically, it looks as if the company will continue to lose cash for the next 21 months but will turn into a positive cash position by the end of 2011 and will develop an increasingly positive cash balance thereafter. All in all, over the next $4^{3/4}$ years the company is expected to generate a positive cash balance of €/£280M.

On this basis it would appear that if the right financing can be put in place it is worth keeping the company going.

The main benefit of doing so for the ordinary shareholders is obviously the fact that they will not receive anything if the company were to be wound up now. However, if the company continues to trade it will grow into a positive net assets position over the medium term, and this should mean that some value will be attributed to the ordinary shares in the company. For example given the current negative net assets breakout value of €/£40M this is projected to be a positive situation of €/£240M by the end of 2013 which should result in some value for the ordinary and preference shareholders. If the company were to be wound up now, neither of these shareholding groups will receive anything.

RISK DECISIONS 89

Solution to Task 18:

The requirement is to ensure that no party in the reconstruction scheme will be worse off than they would be if the company went into liquidation. Therefore, we first of all need to look at the existing parties and see what they would be entitled to in a liquidation

- The 10% Debenture holders will get all their money
- The Other secured loan will also get repaid in full
- 87% of the Bank Overdraft will be repaid
- 87% of trade creditors will be repaid
- The preference shareholders would receive nothing
- The ordinary shareholders would receive nothing

The company needs a cash injection of at least €/£30M to match the deficit for the remaining 9 months in 2009 plus an additional €/£60M for the year ending 2010 (i.e. €/£90M in all).

A possible scheme of reconstruction could be as follows:

First of all, it should be explained to the ordinary and preference shareholders that were Giles Ltd to go into liquidation they would not receive any monies. This should create the desire for both these parties to seek the company's continuance, as they have nothing to gain by it closing down In addition, they would need to be convinced that if the company were to continue to trade, then there is the possibility that there will be value accruing to these shareholders in the years to come. This would be especially crucial if we are to seek new funding from these sources to ensure that Giles Ltd continues to trade.

One possible way to deal with the shareholders is to cancel the existing ordinary shares and preference shares, and issue new shares to obtain the new funding of €/£90M that is required. Giles Ltd may well decide to seek additional funding from ordinary shareholders on top of the €/£90M that is required, as they may want to pay off some of the creditors balances, as the payment days for creditors has begun to slip out over the last number of years. In all, let us say that the ordinary and preference shareholders can be persuaded to give up their current shares and purchase for 200M ordinary €/£1 shares in Giles Ltd at par. This will bring in €/£200M to Giles Ltd as a cash injection immediately. The benefit for Giles Ltd is that it will receive the €/£200M cash and will eliminate the need to pay a preference dividend when they return to profitability. The benefit for the shareholders is that when the company does turn the corner, their shares will become valuable again and allow them to start recouping their investment.

Giles Ltd should also enter discussion with the providers of its bank overdraft, to see if some of the amount owed can be converted into a longer term loan, presumably at a lower interest cost. The benefit for the bank is that if the company continues to trade, and does return to profitability, they will recover the full amount of monies previously advanced. In addition, if the money can be secured on the land and buildings of the company, so that the banks become preferred creditors, this may help alleviate their concerns as to their ability to recover their monies. As well as benefiting from a cheaper rate of interest, the other two big benefits of this renegotiation for Giles Ltd are that firstly it eases their liquidity worries in relation to their ability to meet their debts as they fall due. Secondly, it means that their long-term investments are now being funded by long-term financing, which from a matching perspective is much healthier.

Let's say that in this scenario, as the Land and Buildings are valued at €/£550M Giles Ltd will secure as much long-term debt as possible on these assets. Therefore, they secure the 10% debentures, the existing long-term loans of €/£120M and an additional €/£330M which was in their bank overdraft.

The next group that will need to be satisfied is the debenture holders. Giles Ltd will need to find some way of trying to roll over the debentures or replace the existing debentures with a new issue. The company does not currently have the cash resources to pay back the debenture holders (unless it uses the money from the issue of ordinary shares to do so). One possibility here is that the company rolls over the debentures by re-issuing new five year debentures at a higher rate of interest (say 12%) than at present. For Giles Ltd, the big benefit would be that it delays the need to find cash to repay the debentures for five years, when hopefully the company will be more profitable. Secondly, any extra interest cost should be eliminated by the lower rate payable on the element of the bank overdraft that was transferred into a long-term loan. As the new debentures would once again be secured on the Land & Buildings, their risk has not changed.

Group	Position on liquidation	Position on reconstruction
Debenture Holders	Fully secured	Fully secured with higher interest rate
Secured Loan	Fully secured	Fully secured
Bank Overdraft	87% would be repaid	Introduces security and the prospect of 100% payment
Trade Creditors	87% would be repaid	The prospect of 100% payment
Preference Shareholders	Would receive nothing	The prospect of a return in the future for an investment now
Ordinary Shareholders	Would receive nothing	The prospect of a return in the future for an investment now

Solution to Task 19:

Following reconstruction the Balance sheet will look as follows

Giles Ltd
Reconstructed Balance Sheet

	31.03.09 Reconstructed €/£ M's
Non Current Assets	
Land & Buildings	550
Plant and machinery	70
	620
Current Assets	
Inventory	600
Cash	100
Debtors	70
	770

Current Liabilities

Trade Creditors	400
Bank overdraft (unsecured)	240
	640

Net Current Assets	130
Total Assets Less Current Liabilities	750

Long Term Liabilities

12% debentures 2014 (secured on Land & Buildings)	(100)
Other loans (floating charges)	(450)
	200

Financed By:

Ordinary shares of €/£ 1	200
	200

The reconstructed company would appear to be financially viable on the following basis:

- The debenture holders get an increased rate of interest and maintain their security. Giles Ltd will not have to repay the capital amount in respect of debentures until 2014.

- The company has €/£100M in cash to meet the anticipated cash shortfall of €/£90M for the rest of 2009 and 2010.

- The company has moved €/£330M of funding from short term bank overdraft funding to long term funding. This will better match the source of funding to the use of funding.

- The company has improved its liquidity situation from a Current Ratio of 1.09:1.00 to 1.20:1.00.

- The balance sheet of the company represents the realisable values of the assets and liabilities of Giles Ltd and is therefore now more realistic.

- The company appears well positioned now to repay their debts as they fall due. It will be able to meet the anticipated shortfalls in cash flows for 2009 and 2010 and continue to trade so that it can take advantage of the improving financial performance from 2011 onwards.

- The preference and ordinary shareholders have hope that the company will turn the corner in three years times and that they will get a return on their money. They do have the risk of having to make an investment now, but the prospects going forward do appear quite healthy.

Solution to Task 20:

To: Mary Patterson

Cc: Harry O'Neill

From: James Crown

Re: Sources of Finance available to Giles Ltd

Mary,

I am replying to your request for information in relation to financing for Giles Ltd by outlining the various sources that may be available. Should you require any more information please do not hesitate to contact me.

Regards,

James

LONG-TERM SOURCES OF FINANCE

(i) EQUITY

- *Venture Capital*; As IBRT Ltd has been established for a number of years any capital to be provided by a venture capitalist would be more in the form of development capital rather than seed capital. However, given the future projected profitability of Giles Ltd this may prove an attractive proposition.

- *The Stock Market*; A Full Listing or New Capital Markets for Growing Companies: IEX or AIM. We have already discussed this area with Patrick in relation to IBRT Ltd but would be glad to share that information with you if Patrick is unavailable to do so.

- *Rights Issues*; Effectively the re issue of the ordinary shares and the issue of ordinary shares to the existing preference shareholders is akin to a form of rights issue. Basically, a rights issue is where existing shareholders are invited to purchase new shares in a company on a basis that is proportionate to their existing stake in the company.

- **Retained earnings**; This is not an option for funding at present given the perilous state of Giles Ltd's finances. However, as the company trades out of its difficulties this will become a more viable source of finance long-term.

- **Preference Shares**; The dividends paid on these are not tax deductible, but they do have an advantage over debt in that the dividend amount need not be paid in a period where profit is not earned (although the dividend can be cumulative). Due to the bad experience of the existing preference shareholders there may not be an avenue for Giles Ltd to issue new preference shares.

(ii) DEBT

- **Loan Stock – Debentures**. The company has renegotiated the debentures so that they do not need to be repaid until 2014. A Debenture is a loan where there is a promise to repay the loan amount and associated interest. All debentures carry five characteristics. They carry a maturity term. In the case of Giles Ltd this has been renegotiated to 2014 from 2009. They also carry some security provision. In the case of Giles Ltd the debentures are secured on the land and buildings of the company. They also carry an associated interest rate which will need to be paid each year. In the case of Giles Ltd this was 10% p.a. but has now increased to 12% p.a.. The debentures will usually be denominated in units of €/£1,000 or €/£100. Finally there will be specific provision as to when they will be repaid.

  There are also a number of variations of debentures which I have outlined below.

  - **Zero Coupon Bonds**: these bonds are issued at a discount to the capital value. No interest paid over the life of the bond, because the gain comes in the form of the difference between the discounted issue value and the redemption value. This suits investors who have no desire for an income return but want to earn a capital return.

- **Deep Discount Bonds**: This is similar to zero coupon bonds but here there is interest paid. However, the amount is negligible and the main gain still comes in the form of appreciation of the capital value.

- **Hybrid Sources of Finance**
  - **Convertible Loan Stock**. Here, the lender is given the right to convert the debt into ordinary shares in the firm at specific prices on or before specified dates. This allows the lender to benefit from the performance of the company if the share price rises over time, but offers a safety valve if the company's fortunes disimprove as the lender is entitled to be repaid the capital sum.
  - **Warrants:** In order to raise finance without paying too high a coupon rate, a company will often offer a mix of interest and capital gain potential. Along with interest and a fixed repayment schedule, an investor is also offered an equity sweetener in the form of a warrant. This might be an option for Giles Ltd in order to reduce the proposed debenture interest of 12% going forward.

MEDIUM TERM SOURCES OF FINANCE

- **Leasing**: A lease is a contractual agreement whereby the owner of an asset (lessor) allows another party (lessee) economic ownership of that asset for a specified period of time. Lease agreements are offered by most financial institutions, such as banks and insurance companies.

- **Hire Purchase**: With hire purchase, ownership remains with the seller until the last instalment is paid (subject to certain rules). The agreement usually covers the rental of goods and has an option to purchase at the end of the hire purchase term at a nominal price. This differs from a credit sale agreement which transfers ownership immediately to the purchaser who agrees to pay for the goods over a specified period.

- **Bank Loans**: A bank loan is usually for a fixed period of time with payments of interest and principal on an agreed periodic basis. They are generally tailored to suit the individual requirements of the business.

SHORT TERM SOURCES OF FINANCE

- *Bank Overdraft*: This is a source widely used by businesses especially as a cash cushion (i.e., if a company for whatever reason is caught short of cash it will use its overdraft facility to cover the situation). Bank overdrafts are intended to meet specific short-term financing needs. Their main disadvantage is that they can be a costly source of debt and are technically repayable on demand. In this case Giles Ltd looks to have an over reliance on their bank overdraft to fund their activities (including long-term investments which goes against the 'matching principle') and the reconstruction should address this fact.

- *Delay of Payments*: These are sources which arise through the normal course of business and usually the user has to do nothing in order to access the funds. They will include things like delaying payments to creditors and tax returns. Overuse of this form of financing could have knock-on implications for Giles Ltd, in that it may affect the security of supply for key services and products provided by the vendor base. In addition the Taxation Authorities will apply quite onerous penalty charges for delays in making returns.

ASSET BACKED FINANCE

- *Factoring:* Factoring involves the outright sale of a company's accounts receivable to a financial institution called a factor. The factor will take over the debt collection process of the company (this may be with or without recourse). They will agree to advance a percentage value of a debtors at a specified date, and will charge a fee and a financing charge in respect of the service. In addition, they may offer insurance against bad debts and may also provide assistance in relation to credit assessment and credit control procedures.

- *Sale and Leaseback*: Here a company will sell one of its long-term assets (usually land and / or buildings) to a financial institution and then lease it back from them. This frees up a valuable resource on the balance sheet of the company and turns it into a finance source. A major issue for Giles Ltd in doing this would appear to be the fact that their long-term assets such as land and buildings are already being used to secure both the debentures and the long term loans and therefore may not be available to take part in such a financing option.

GOVERNMENT ASSISTED FINANCE

There are a multitude of grants available from the various government agencies in respect of businesses that are either looking for ongoing or start-up financing. Given the likelihood that Giles Ltd may be about to close, the possibility of the government providing funding would be greatly increased.

Solution to Task 21:

To: Harry O'Neill

From: James Crown

Re: Main causes of business failure and early warning signs

Harry,

There are generally considered to be five different sources of information in terms of the identification of business failure. While none of these are definitive in their own right, and some organisations which are destined to fail may not exhibit all these symptoms, they do nonetheless provide a good starting point. I have included a brief summary of these issues below and would be happy to discuss them with you at your convenience,

Regards,

James

(i) Scientific Approaches

- Ratio analysis is concerned with the efficiency and effectiveness of an organisation's use resources and the financial stability of that organisation. The main ratios that are used as predictors of business failure tend to be the current or quick ratios and where these are well below 2:1 or 1:1 respectively, they may be seen as indicators of financial difficulties

- The scientific approach tends to try and use predictive modelling to identify possible cases of business failure. Altman developed a model based on assigning various values to financial ratios associated with a company, ultimately arriving at a 'Z Score' which, depending on the score achieved in the model, predicts the likelihood of the business failing or not.

- There are some issues with the use of Z Scores, in that the model was based on a small number of US companies, and it is not transferable as a model to private companies where the market value of equity may be difficult to obtain. However, they do tend to be used in the banking and accountancy sectors.

(ii) Accounting Information based approach

- The accounts will give a history of whether the company is profitable or not, and the bottom line is that while a company can sustain periods of unprofitability, if it manages it's cash position well in the long-run an organisation has to be somewhat profitable if it is going to survive. Likewise, companies may experience difficulties even when they are profitable, if they do not manage their cash resources properly. Peter Drucker in his article *'Cash is King'* notes that organisations might not go into liquidation because they are not profitable, but will do so if they cannot manage their cash so that they can pay their debts as they fall due.

- Typically, the main thing that accounts provide is information on the financial health of the company at a point in time. Therefore, they will include Balance Sheets, Income and Expenditure Statements, Cash flow statements, director's reports, auditor's reports, as well as detailed notes relating to the accounts. From this one can build a picture as to the historical and current performance of organisations.

- The main criticism of accounting information is that it does not provide a complete picture of the organisation, in that it is focused primarily on financial information. Therefore, in order to develop a more complete view as to the performance of an organisation, one may have to access information relating to non-financial areas of a business, such as staff morale and turnover, customer satisfaction, environmental issues, key customers, impending legislation that may affect the company etc. In addition, one should also recognise the fact that accounting information is historical in nature and the balance sheet provides information at a point in time so their predictive ability may be questionable.

(iii) Management Deficiencies

- There is a view that business failure is something that emerges as a result of inefficient management. John Argenti maintains that where senior management expertise is inadequate across all the areas of the business, and where corporate planning is poor, this may create issues for an organisation. These issues can then be compounded by the lack of an accurate and timely financial management system that provides incorrect or out-of-date information.

- Once these deficiencies are in place, the company may continue to trade, but it becomes very susceptible to making a major mistake such as overtrading, over gearing or launching a major project that it too big for the organisation to manage effectively given their abilities.

- These issues then lead on to create a number of symptoms of corporate failure, namely the use of 'creative accounting', deterioration of the company's financial position and customer focus as well as a desperate search for capital.

(iv) Casual Observation

- Other issues that may emerge which begin to indicate the possible failure of an organisation can include a deterioration in the ability of the company to pay their creditors, a product portfolio which is dependent on products coming to the end of their life cycle or patent, key staff leaving the organisation and a lack of up-to-date information.

(v) Other Published information

- Sometimes it may be possible to glean a lot about the health of an organisation from other sources of information that are published, such as information in the published accounts, the reports of directors and the chairman, newspaper articles, and published information about other things that may impact on the company's ability to trade successfully in the future, such as legislation or environmental issues.

Solution Task 22:

To: Harry O'Neill

From: James Crown

Re: Risk Management

Harry,

As requested I have done some research into what is meant by risk management. Please see my analysis below.

Regards,

James

What is Risk?

Risk is the threat that an event, action or failure to act will adversely affect an organisation's ability to achieve its objectives and to successfully execute its strategies. Risks are events or conditions that are not certain to happen, but if they were to happen, they would have undesirable consequences for the organisation.

Risk Management

Risk management is a process of clearly defined steps which support better decision making by contributing a greater insight into risks and their impacts. It incorporates proactive decisions and actions for continually assessing, ranking and prioritising risk, and implementing various strategies to mitigate or control risk. It is the process whereby organisations address the risks attaching to their activities, with the goal of achieving sustained benefit within each activity and across the portfolio of all activities.

Risk Mission Statement

IBRT Ltd should have a risk mission statement which would provide a framework to identify, rate and manage risk in order to provide reasonable assurance that the strategic objectives of the company can be achieved.

Solution Task 23:

To: harryoneill@sonner&saville.com

From: Jamescrown@sonner&saville.com

Re: Different types of risk an organisation can face

Harry,

As requested please see below a summary of the different types of risk that an organisation may face. Some risks will be unique to IBRT Ltd, but at least this will give Patrick an idea of how to categorise the company's risks.

- *Financial Risk* is the risk that an organisation may not be able to meet its financial obligations. It includes risks relating to the procedures, systems and accounting records in place to ensure that the organisation is not exposed to avoidable financial risks, including risks to assets. An example would be the improper use of funds. Other types of financial risks that a company might face would be foreign exchange exposures, interest rate exposures, gearing problems and significant projects that create a financial burden on a company etc.

- *Operational Risks* are risks relating to the procedures and technologies employed to achieve particular objectives. IT problems, problems with manufacturing equipment, access to skilled labour etc. would be examples.

- *Reputational Risks* involve risk to the public reputation of the organisation and its effects. Examples of these can be the company's Health & Safety record, environmental record etc.

- *Strategic Risks* are risks that may be external to the organisation such as the economic climate, oil price fluctuations, exchange rate movements, interest rates and inflation.

Regards,

James

Solution Task 24:

To: harryoneill@sonner&saville.com

From: Jamescrown@sonner&saville.com

Re: Risk management Policy

Harry,

As requested, please see below the steps that IBRT Ltd can take to manage their risks more effectively;

Regards,

James

Step 1: Identify Risks

Identifying risk is the key to the success of a risk management process, as all other elements of the process flow from this initial step. It is crucial that a thorough job of risk identification is accomplished on a regular basis. There are basically four risk categories that need to be identified (ie Financial, Operational, Reputational & Strategic).

Organisations can use a variety of techniques to identify risk including the following;

- Listing the obvious risks
- Brainstorming (when, where, why and how are risks likely to arise)
- Questionnaires
- Workshops
- Incident investigations
- Audits and inspections
- Cost benefit analysis
- SWOT analysis
- Sensitivity analysis
- Cash flow analysis
- Decision trees

Step 2: Assessing Risks

When risks have been identified, the next step is to assess them. Risk should be assessed using two criteria;

- *The Impact on the Organisation* if the risk factor actually occurs will be estimated using a scale of 1 to 5 as follows
  1 = No significant impact
  2 = Minor impact
  3 = Significant but containable impact
  4 = High impact
  5 = Extremely detrimental effect.

- *The Likelihood of the Risk Occurring* will also be estimated using a scale of 1 to 5 as follows
  1 = Rarely if ever
  2 = Possible
  3 = Likely
  4 = Very Likely
  5 = Almost unavoidable/already occurring.

A risk score (risk rating) is determined by multiplying the results of the two criteria together. IBRT Ltd will then decide a cut off score, above which risks are significant, and as much work as possible needs to go into ensuring that the risks will not materialise. Scores below the cut off point are not significant and need to be monitored, but not acted on unless they become significant.

Step 3: Addressing Risk

When risks have been identified and assessed and the controls in place are not deemed adequate, then each responsible area in the organisation should determine an appropriate method for addressing them. Taking action to reduce the impact or likelihood of a risk occurring is referred to as mitigating the risk.

To begin with, existing controls should be examined to determine whether they are adequate and appropriate. Existing controls should be recorded when individual areas in the organisation are completing risk returns for input into the Risk Register (see below).

It is also important to remember that there should be a balance between mitigation of risk and the costs of any action taken. Each area should ensure that the costs of controls to mitigate risk are not disproportionate to the reduction in the potential impact or likelihood of the risk.

There are a number of approaches to risk mitigation including;

- Risk reduction
- Risk transfer
- Risk avoidance

Risk Reduction strategies are used to contain risk to an acceptable level. The objective is not necessarily to prevent the risk totally, but rather to contain it to an acceptable level. Risk reduction strategies will aim to minimise the frequency and/or severity of the negative impacts of a risk. An example is the preparation of contingency plans to expedite recovery from losses.

Risk Transfer is where an organisation will effectively pass the risk onto another entity. The most common form of this is insurance, or the contracting out of services to a best-in-class service provider.

Risk Avoidance involves decisions not to undertake activities or programmes.

Step 4: Evaluating Risk Controls

The effectiveness of the risk controls or risk mitigating actions put in place to address risks, should be kept under regular review by each area within IBRT Ltd. Each area is asked to state whether the controls in place to mitigate risk are;

A. Highly effective
B. Effective
C. Not effective

The ongoing resources assigned or required to address risk should also be analysed under this heading.

Step 5: Reporting and Monitoring of Risks

Reporting of risks in the Company should be facilitated by the risk liaison officer/unit. (RLO). Each area within IBRT Ltd should be required to make returns to the risk liaison officer at regular intervals (e.g. quarterly). The RLO will maintain a risk register and should prepare quarterly reports to Executive Management based on the Risk Returns. This should be a formal agenda item for Executive Management on a regular basis.

Step 6: Risk Register

The Risk Register is a recording of all risks facing IBRT Ltd and is an active document prepared from detail provided by each area in the company. This should be maintained centrally by the Risk Liaison Officer and should be updated from risk returns made by each area and signed off by a member of the Executive team.

Solution Task 25:

To: Harry O'Neill

From: James Crown

Re: Treasury Function

Harry,

Please see below the information relating to a centralised Treasury function.

Roles of a treasury department

- Centralised Banking co-ordination
- Management of an organisation's Risk Policy
- Centralised sourcing of funds
- Co-ordination of Insurance
- Management of Foreign currency exposures
- Interest rate risk management
- Maintenance of the Corporate finance function

Advantages of a centralised treasury department

- As the company has consolidated all its cash centrally, it may be able to obtain more favourable interest rates on its deposits because it has larger lump sums to invest
- Lower rates of interest may be achieved for borrowing due to the consolidation of borrowing requirements

106 STRATEGIC FINANCE AND MANAGEMENT ACCOUNTING TOOLKIT

- Expertise in the area of treasury management can be clustered centrally and can eliminate dilution of expertise.
- For organisations that trade in foreign currencies, it is much easier to integrate together hedging strategies involving the matching of receipt and payment currencies, leading and lagging payments, remittance of cash effectively etc.
- Safety cash balances that need to be kept on hand can be minimised as any amount needed can be held centrally

Solution Task 26:

To:	Patrick Murphy
From:	James Crown
Cc:	Harry O'Neill
Date:	7th March 2009
Re:	Different Types of Currency Risk

Patrick,

Following your discussion with Mr. Harry O'Neill on March 5th 2009, I have detailed below the three main types of currency risks (Also called Exposures) associated with transacting in International markets.

(a) **Transaction Exposure:** This is the risk that a firm will gain or lose in the course of normal trading transactions due to movements in exchange rates. This is a cash-flow exposure. When an organisation trades internationally the amount of €/£'s paid or received may vary from that envisaged when the initial agreement was made. This is because foreign exchange rates fluctuate and may change between the agreement date and the payment date.

(b) **Translation Exposure:** This arises in respect of differences in currencies in which assets and liabilities are de-nominated, and relates to a loss or gain in valuation between two particular points in time. Therefore, when an organisation has a foreign subsidiary and translates the accounts of that foreign subsidiary into the parent's currency, exchange rate movements may cause the value of the assets and liabilities of that subsidiary to vary from previous translations

(c) **Economic Exposure:** This is the effect of international exchange rate movements on the competitiveness of an organisation. It should be stressed that this exposure is very much a long-term one. It differs from the first two types of exposure identified above, as this may affect an organisation that does not deal in foreign markets at all. Take the example of an Irish/UK company that buys its inputs in the eurozone/UK, and the US Dollar weakens against the Euro/Sterling. It may be cheaper for the Company to switch its purchasing from Europe/UK to the US, as it can get its inputs cheaper. In this instance, foreign exchange rate movements favour the buying company but weaken the market position of an exporting/selling company in the euro zone/ UK.

If you have any questions on this please do not hesitate to contact me

James

Solution Task 27:

Definition of a Forward Contract Rate of Exchange

A forward exchange contract is an immediately firm and binding contract between a bank and a customer for the purchase or sale of a specified quantity of a stated foreign currency. The rate of exchange is fixed at the time the contract is made, for performance at a future time agreed upon when making the contract. A forward rate is determined by the relationship between the interest rates of two countries. The currency of the country with the higher interest rate should weaken vis-à-vis the country with the lower interest rate. This is called the Theory of Interest Rate Parity.

Calculation of a Forward Rate of Exchange

A Forward rate is therefore calculated as the spot rate on the day a forward exchange contract is made, plus or minus the interest rate differential for the period of the contract.

Current spot rate $\qquad = \qquad$ \$1.57 to €/£1.00.

The forward exchange rate is calculated as:

$$\text{Current Spot rate} \times \frac{1 + (\text{USD Interest rate} \times 1\text{month}/12 \text{ months})}{1 + (\text{Euro/Sterling Interest rate} \times 1\text{month}/12 \text{ months})}$$

$$= \quad \$1.57 \quad \times \quad \frac{1.00333}{1.00250} \quad = \quad \$1.57 \times 1.000828 \quad = \quad \$1.5713$$

Conclusion

- IBRT Ltd will receive €/£63,641 (ie \$100,000/1.5713) on April 15th using this rate.

- IBRT Ltd will receive €/£62,500 in a month's time at a rate of \$1.60 to €/£1.00, which has been offered by the bank.

- Therefore the rate of \$1.60 to €/£1.00 would not appear to be a good forward contract rate. Patrick should shop around.

Solution Task 28: Using the Money Market

- **How much USD to borrow now:**

  We need to calculate the amount of USD we need to borrow on March 15th so that when interest is added for one month, it will equate to \$100,000 on April 15th.

  With the USD lending rate at 8% p.a., this implies that the one-month lending rate is 0.666 of 1% (ie 8% / 12 months).

  Therefore in order to owe \$100,000 in one month's time it will be necessary to borrow \$99,338 now (ie \$100,000 / 1.00666).

What is the value of that USD amount in €/£'s on March 15th

We take this figure of \$99,338 which we borrow on March 15th and translate into Euros/Sterling at the spot rate of \$1.57 to €/£1.00 on March 15th.

This would result in IBRT Ltd realising €/£63,272 on March 15th

RISK DECISIONS   109

Solution Task 29: Using the Option Contract

- A Value of $100,000 converted into Euros/Sterling at the option rate of $1.56 to €/£1.00 on April 15th 2009 is €/£64,103.

- €/£64,103 receivable on April 15th discounted to present value on March 15th (using the €/£ one month deposit rate of 25% (ie 3% annual rate)) is €/£63,943.

- The value to IBRT Ltd of the sale by trading on the money market, as identified in Task 28 is €/£63,272 on March 15th.

- The difference between the values calculated under the option contract (€/£63,943) and that under the money market (€/£63,272) is €/£671. This is the maximum premium that IBRT Ltd. should be prepared to pay for the option contract.

Solution Task 30: Using Futures

If IBRT Ltd goes ahead with the sale of the Futures on March 15th it means that they will sell 10 USD futures @ $10,000 each. They will then close out this futures position on April 15[th]by buying 10 USD Futures. If the USD has weakened, there will be a profit on the futures position (as the buying price of the USD Futures will be lower than what they were sold at previously) which will offset the lower €/£ value they will get for the sale proceeds. If the USD strengthens, there will be a loss on the futures position but the company will receive more Euros/Sterling from their USD sale.

Solution Task 31: Currency Swap

The most obvious solution here is a currency swap. This is where two parties agree to swap equivalent amounts of currency for a period.

- IBRT Ltd knows that it will receive a cheque for $100,000 on April 15th. The US Multi-national knows that it will receive €/£63,694 (ie $100,000 at the March 15th rate of $1.57 to €/£1.00) on April 15th. However neither can be sure what the value will be in their reporting currency when they try and translate back into local currency on April 15th. To introduce certainty into the transactions IBRT Ltd can agree to swap their receipt (of $100,000) with the US Multi-national's receipt (of €/£63,694). This brings certainty into the March transactions for both parties in terms of the money they will receive.

- The receipt of €/£63,694 is on April 15th. We can calculate the March 15th equivalent amount by adjusting for the Euro/UK deposit rate. This gives a value of €/£63,535 on the transaction at March 15th (€/£63,694 / 1.0025) which is the present value of the amount that IBRT Ltd. Will receive.

Solution Task 32:

To: Patrick Murphy

From: James Crown (Sonner & Saville)

Cc: Harry O'Neill

Date: 8th January 2009

Re: Interest Rate Exposure & Managing a Debt Portfolio

Patrick,

Interest rate Exposure:

Interest rate exposure typically occurs where an organisation has a level of debt or savings that leaves it vulnerable to movements in interest rates. As a general rule there are four ways in which a company can be vulnerable to changes in interest rates:

(a) If a company has fixed rate savings, they may lose out on potential interest income if interest rates rise;

(b) If a company has variable rate savings, they may lose out if interest rates fall;

(c) If a company has fixed rate borrowing, they may end up paying more interest than is necessary if interest rates fall; and

(d) If a company has variable rate borrowings they may lose out if interest rates rise.

Generally, organisations will try and assess the magnitude of the interest cash flows vis-à-vis their overall cash flows. If they deem these to be significant they may then decide to take steps to try and minimise their exposure to interest rate changes.

Managing a Debt Portfolio:

There are three areas that need to be taken into account by an organisation in managing their Debt Portfolios;

(a) **Maturity Mix:** Organisations should stagger the dates when debts become liable for repayment / renegotiation. In this way they avoid having to renegotiate all their debt at one point in time, which can be difficult and time consuming. If the money has to be repaid, they avoid having to find the cash for repayment all in one go.

(b) **The Matching Principle:** Organisations should try to match their assets and liabilities as well as possible, when both have a near common interest rate. For banks this would mean matching the interest received from borrowers to the interest paid to depositors.

(c) **The Mix of Fixed and Variable Rate Debt:** An organisation should try to balance this mix use of this, because if they hold too much fixed rate debt they will lose out if interest rates fall. If they hold too much floating rate debt they will lose out if interest rates rise.

If you have any questions on this please do not hesitate to contact me.

Regards

James

Solution Task 33: Managing Interest Rate Exposures

An interest rate swap would appear to be the best possibility for the two companies. IBRT Ltd has a preference for variable rate debt but is not prepared to pay a higher rate for it than what it can access fixed rate debt for. CME, on the other hand, can access variable rate debt at a cheaper rate than fixed rate debt but it actually wants fixed rate debt.

The following is an example of a swap that could be arranged that might suit both parties.

- IBRT Ltd borrows at a fixed rate of 6.25% from its bank.
- CME borrows at a variable rate of 6.75% from First Bank PLC.
- Both companies agree to swap their interest repayments, such that CME will pay IBRT Ltd's fixed rate payments and IBRT Ltd will pay CME Ltd's variable payments.
- IBRT Ltd agrees to pay CME 6.50% in respect of the swap, and CME agrees to pay IBRT 6.75% in respect of the swap

IBRT Ltd			CME Ltd		
Pays:	The Bank	- 6.25%	Pays:	The Bank	- 6.75%
	CME Ltd	- 6.50%		IBRT Ltd	- 6.75%
Receives	CME Ltd	6.75%	Receives	IBRT Ltd	6.50%
Total Cost		**6.00%**	**Total Cost**		**6.50%**

Both organizations are now clearly better off. IBRT Ltd is now paying variable interest @ 6% which is a full half percent better than they could have achieved themselves directly with the bank. CME Ltd is also better off as they now have access to fixed rate debt at a rate that is a full three-quarters of a percent cheaper than they could have accessed directly with First Bank PLC.

RISK DECISIONS   113

Solution 34:

To: Patrick Murphy

From: James Crown

Cc: Harry O'Neill

Date: 12th April 2009

Re: Interest rate forward rate agreements and interest rate options

Patrick,

I have outlined below a brief description of interest rate forward rate agreements and interest rate options, and how they might be of assistance to you in managing your interest rate exposures

(a) Forward rate agreements;

This is an agreement that IBRT Ltd would enter into with its bank which would agree the interest rate that will be apply to a loan to be taken out at a future point in time. This will allow IBRT Ltd to know today what rate of interest it will pay on any borrowings it takes out at a future point in time, and therefore brings certainty into the future cash flows associated with financing a particular project or investment. Of course, if interest rates fall, IBRT Ltd will not benefit from lower interest payments as they have locked into a fixed rate. Likewise, IBRT Ltd will be protected if interest rates move upwards.

In this case, I would advise you to discuss IBRT Ltd's future borrowing requirements with the bank, and the timeframe for same. You will then be in a position to negotiate a forward rate interest rate agreement to cover the amounts borrowed. One point that I would note is that the Board of IBRT Ltd expect interest rates to fall in the future, so in entering into any forward rate agreement, one would expect to do so at an interest rate lower than what currently exists in the marketplace.

(b) Interest Rate Option;

An Interest rate option differs slightly from a forward rate agreement in that it would offer IBRT Ltd the right (but not the obligation) to borrow a sum of money from their bank, at an agreed future date and at an agreed rate of interest. Typically, this will cost more than a forward rate agreement, as all the downside risk resides with the bank if the interest rate rises above the option rate, IBRT Ltd will exercise their option to pay interest at the lower options rate, and the bank is liable for the difference. If interest rates fall below the option rate, IBRT Ltd will not exercise their option and the bank will lose out on the possibility of receiving higher interest.

Regards,

James

Solution to Task 35:

To: harryoneill@sonner&saville.com

From: Jamescrown@sonner&saville.com

Re: Value at Risk

Harry,

As discussed, I have done some research into the concept of Value at Risk (VAR).

- Value at Risk is a concept that was developed in the 1990's in order to help organisations to quantify their risk. Basically, VAR represents the maximum amount that an organisation can lose over a specific time period. It is used extensively by pension funds, and to a growing degree by companies and financial institutions.
- VAR involves looking at all of the potential exposures that are facing an organisation at a particular point in time, and trying to quantify them. These could include currency and interest rate exposures we have looked at previously in relation to IBRT Ltd. However, these exposures can also extend to liquidity exposures, investment decisions, financing decisions, gearing, and operational risk among others.
- VAR has gained credence over the last number of years in response to a number of high profile risk management failures, including the AIB bank losses in the US and Baring's bank in Singapore.

- In terms of being of use to IBRT Ltd, I would suggest that we should discuss VAR in more detail with Patrick, as the above is only a very brief summary of the concept. We would need to see if the amount of work necessary to implement a VAR system for IBRT Ltd would be warranted.

Regards,

James

TOPIC FOUR
PERFORMANCE MEASUREMENT

PERFORMANCE MEASUREMENT

The final topic to be studied as part of Paper 2: Strategic Finance and Management Accounting – Performance Measurement, will now be reviewed. The textbook accompanying this case study topic is, "Managerial Accounting: Costing, Decision Making & Control" by Peter Clarke (2008), The Institute of Chartered Accountants in Ireland. At the conclusion of this, you should be able to successfully complete each of the following tasks under the five headings outlined below;

- Framework for performance measurement
  - Explain the functioning of:
    - Controls within the organisation
    - Management accounting control systems
    - Responsibility centres
  - Demonstrate an understanding of Contingency Theory

- Performance measurement decisions (*Please refer to Chapter's 7, 8 & 10)
  - Evaluate performance, including: product evaluation, business unit performance, consideration of non-financial indicators, environmental issues and ethical dimensions
  - Outline the use of Key Performance Indicators (KPIs), the balanced scorecard and other developments in management accounting
  - Advise on the use of advanced financial analysis and benchmarking as a means of improving management accounting systems and business processes
  - Analyse the practical issues which arise when using performance measures

120 STRATEGIC FINANCE AND MANAGEMENT ACCOUNTING TOOLKIT

- ○ Identify organisation strategy, goals and targets and design appropriate performance measures. Explain how they may be used to assist achieve the organisation's goals
- ○ Demonstrate a detailed understanding of the typical performance measurement conflicts (short term vs. long term, financial vs. non-financial and quantified vs. non-quantified)
- Advanced Variance Analysis (***Please refer to Chapter 15**)
  - ○ Explain the role of variance analysis in performance measurement
  - ○ Determine planning and operating variances and be able to interpret the results of this analysis

- Divisional performance measures and ethics (***Please refer to Chapter 16**)
  - ○ Distinguish between the alternative centres for departmental and divisional performance (cost, revenue, profit and investment centres) including how they are assessed and monitored
  - ○ Differentiate between centralised and decentralised decision-making approaches
  - ○ Advise of the advantages and limitations of divisionalisation
  - ○ Compare alternative performance measures, to include: profit, ROCE, residual income and economic value added
  - ○ Calculate and advise on the most appropriate measure(s) for a given scenario
  - ○ Explain the possible dysfunctional consequences of using short term measures
  - ○ Recognise and explain the potential ethical dilemmas which can occur in the management of divisional performance

- Transfer Pricing (***Please refer to Chapter 16**)
  - ○ Explain the context of transfer pricing
  - ○ Identify and explain the following issues involved in transfer pricing; aims, approaches and possible conflicts
  - ○ Explain and advise on the alternative approaches available in setting transfer prices to include; the cost based methods, the market based method and the negotiated method
  - ○ Identify potential or existing sources of conflict and advise on resolution strategies

PERFORMANCE MEASUREMENT   121

A number of weeks later, Harry e-mails you and requests that you attend a meeting with him at 9am in his office the following morning. At this meeting, Harry is visibly delighted to inform you that he has recently recruited a new and prestigious client called Murphy Ltd for Sonner, Saville & Co. Chartered Accountants. This firm (Murphy Ltd) is based in Ireland and specialises in the production of electrical components for use in the automotive sector. Harry informs you that the Board of Directors of Murphy Ltd have ambitious expansion plans for the firm, and to this end, they have recently acquired all of the share capital of a competitor Irish firm called Smith Ltd for a significant cash consideration. Based on projected synergies, they believe that this acquisition will allow them to compete with their larger European rivals on a more competitive and cost effective basis.

The Managing Director of Murphy Ltd, Mr. Declan Barry, had previously been a client of Sonner & Saville while working for another firm, and was extremely happy with the levels of service and professionalism provided. According to Harry, Declan regards performance measurement as imperative to the successful operation of any business, and as a result he is eager to attain the best possible advice in this area. Also, the fact that a number of Murphy Ltd's prominent shareholders have voiced their concerns about the amount paid for Smith Ltd, has convinced Declan of the need to ensure that Murphy Ltd is adequately equipped to deal with the various performance measurement issues that will invariably arise in the future to enable them to extract the maximum value possible from their current and future portfolio of investments. Therefore, the services of Sonner & Saville have been engaged to advise Declan and the Board of Directors of Murphy Ltd in this regard.

Harry informs you that the recruitment of Murphy Ltd is a great coup for Sonner & Saville, as many of their competitors were also proactively seeking to capture this potentially lucrative business. However, as the firm's Corporate Finance Partner for the last number of years, Harry readily admits that he needs to reacquaint himself with the whole area of performance measurement and management accounting control systems prior to offering advice to Murphy Ltd. Therefore, as your first task, Harry asks you to draft a report for him outlining a framework for performance measurement that will form the basis for the firm's future dealings with Murphy Ltd. Before leaving his office, Harry also suggests that you familiarise yourself with some of the key concepts in the area of performance measurement as he expects you to be heavily involved with Murphy Ltd over the coming weeks and months.

> **Task 36: Within the context of a performance measurement system, draft a report to Harry which explains the functioning of: controls within an organisation, management accounting control systems and responsibility centres.**

A couple of days later, Harry telephones you and tells you that as a result of reading your report, he is beginning to think in performance measurement terms once again. However, since your last conversation, Harry has discussed the acquisition of Murphy Ltd and the likely resource implications for Sonner & Saville at their weekly senior management meeting. During the course of these discussions, John Keane, the firm's Audit Partner, congratulated Harry on the acquisition of Murphy Ltd as a client for the firm, but also stressed the importance of considering contingency theory in any performance measurement scenario. As Harry is due to commence a week's family holiday that evening, he asks you to draft a memorandum for him examining this area as well as finalising a number of audit files that you're currently working on.

> **Task 37: Draft a memorandum for Harry outlining what is meant by contingency theory within the context of performance measurement.**

Upon his return from holiday, you receive a telephone call from Harry asking you to meet him in his office later that afternoon. Here, Harry tells you that he has read your memorandum on contingency theory and now appreciates the importance of this area from a performance measurement perspective as previously advocated by John Keane.

On that topic, Harry tells you that he spoke with Declan Barry that morning, who informed him that he, along with a number of his colleagues in Murphy Ltd are currently conducting an operating review of the past and projected performance of Smith Ltd. Based upon their initial findings, Declan is concerned about the recent performance and future viability of a key product manufactured by Smith Ltd called "XY123". According to Declan, Smith Ltd's management team are convinced that this product has been loss-making for a number of years and are also projecting a loss for the coming financial year. On that basis, they are recommending that this product should be discontinued immediately. Although they also "appear" to have the accounting information to support their argument; Declan is sceptical and has asked Harry to advise him in this regard.

Harry tells you that he has asked Declan to source and e-mail him all of the relevant information for the coming financial year pertaining to this particular product. As Declan is eager for a full financial analysis as soon as possible, Harry has promised to deliver his findings by the middle of the following week.

However, Harry then informs you that as he is due to attend a conference for the latter part of the week examining the current state of Corporate Governance in Ireland, hosted by the Institute of Chartered Accountants in Ireland, he wants you to review the figures to be sent by Declan and based upon your analysis, to provide him with an initial recommendation as to whether the product should be discontinued. Harry will then review your results before informing Declan of the outcome.

Armed with this request, you head back to your desk and await the figures from Harry. Soon afterwards Harry telephones you and tells you that he has just forwarded on the information that he has received from Declan but that if you have questions for him while at the conference, he can be contacted via his Blackberry. On opening the e-mail from Harry, the following information was provided in respect of product "XY123" for the coming financial year (all figures in €/£);

Sales Revenue	1,200,000
Direct Materials	(750,000)
Direct Labour	(360,000)
Production Overheads	(200,000)
Depreciation	(150,000)
Electricity	(75,000)
Insurance	(50,000)
Rent & Rates	(45,000)
Supervisor's Salary	(80,000)
Marketing	(60,000)
Administration	(75,000)
General Expenses	(90,000)
Projected Loss	**(735,000)**

You have also been provided with the following additional information;

1. Half of the direct materials needed to produce this product are already in stock, but if they're not used to produce "XY123", they could be sold to a rival firm immediately for €/£250,000. The remainder of the materials will need to be purchased from the firm's usual supplier at the standard price.

2. The direct labour cost consists of expenses relating to both full-time and part-time employees. Four full-time employees work solely on this product and are paid €/£50,000 each per annum. If this product was discontinued, two of these employees would be made redundant immediately while the other two are expected to take up employment opportunities elsewhere within the firm. The remainder of the direct labour expense relates to part-time employees, who would be made redundant if the product was discontinued. The firm has been advised by their legal advisors that on the basis of European Union (EU) labour laws, all production employees (including supervisors) made redundant are entitled to a payment of 8/52 of their projected annual salary for the coming year, payable immediately.

3. Two thirds of the production overheads are regarded as variable, with the remainder fixed.

4. The depreciation expense relates to production machinery used solely to produce "XY123".

5. The firm estimates that three quarters of the electricity expense is incurred in the production of this product, while the remainder represents an allocation of Smith Ltd's overall electricity bill.

6. Half of the insurance expense is directly related to the production of "XY123", while the remainder is split evenly between two other products manufactured by Smith Ltd, both of which are regarded as complementary to "XY123", and for accounting purposes is charged to "XY123".

7. Management estimate that one quarter of the rent and rates expense could be avoided if the production of "XY123" was discontinued.

8. One supervisor is employed on a full-time basis to oversee the production of "XY123". However, if this product is discontinued, this employee has indicated to senior management that they intend to leave the firm immediately.

9. Two thirds of the marketing cost relates directly to "XY123", while the remainder is an allocation of the firm's expenses in promoting the sale of the two complementary products.

10. Smith Ltd employs two administrative staff in respect of "XY123", both of whom are paid equally. In the event that the product is discontinued, the firm expects to retain these employees.

11. General expenses are allocated to products on the basis of floor area occupied. It is estimated by management that 80% of these expenses would still be incurred even if a decision is taken to discontinue "XY123".

> **Task 38: Based upon the information provided, draft a report outlining whether product "XY123" should be discontinued. Round all figures to the nearest whole number and state clearly any assumptions that you make.**

On returning from the conference, Harry telephones you and tells you that he has reviewed your analysis and concurs with your recommendation. However, notwithstanding the results of the financial analysis; Harry thinks that it would be prudent for Declan to consider some non-financial factors before making a final decision as to the continued viability of "XY123". He therefore suggests that you prepare a memorandum for him outlining the range of non-financial, environmental and ethical issues that Declan should consider, which he will then amalgamate with the financial analysis before distributing to Declan.

> **Task 39: Draft a memorandum outlining the non-financial, environmental and ethical issues that Declan should consider before making a final decision as to the continued viability of "XY123".**

A few days later, Declan telephones Harry and is very complementary about the comprehensive analysis produced in respect of "XY123". He tells Harry that he had a "gut" feeling about the performance of this product and that your results have confirmed his suspicions. He will now present these findings to the senior management of Smith Ltd at their next scheduled meeting, and based upon your analysis, he will recommend that the product should not be discontinued but instead should become a key component of Smith Ltd's competitive strategy in the future. Harry is delighted with this outcome as he believes that it will re-enforce Murphy Ltd's decision to engage the services of Sonner, Saville & Co. Chartered Accountants.

At the conclusion of their telephone conversation, Declan tells Harry that he met a former colleague recently, Sarah Jones, who now works as a Management Consultant for a top accountancy firm based in Dublin. After discussing the whereabouts of former employees, the conversation turned to work matters, and specifically the whole area of performance management. While admitting that many firms still relied predominantly on financial metrics when making critical business decisions, Sarah informed Declan that there are now a range of new developments in management accounting designed to facilitate management decision-making in the performance measurement domain.

As Declan is not overly familiar with many of the recent developments in management accounting, he asks Harry to prepare a report for him outlining these techniques as he feels that some of them may be useful to Murphy Ltd in the future. As Harry knows that you completed a project in your final year at University on the topic of the Balanced Scorecard, he asks you to begin this process.

Task 40: Draft a report for Harry outlining the use of Key Performance Indicators (KPIs), the balanced scorecard and other developments in management accounting.

Having completed this task, you e-mail your report to Harry who responds by requesting that the two of you meet up in his office that afternoon to discuss it. At this meeting, Harry tells you that apart from a few minor changes which he has highlighted, your report is very comprehensive and thorough and is practically ready to be sent to Declan.

Concerning another matter, Harry tells you that although Declan was delighted with the financial and non-financial analysis pertaining to "XY123", he has indicated to Harry that he has become increasingly concerned with the current state of Smith Ltd's management accounting systems and business processes. Indeed, Declan believes that the initial decision reached by Smith Ltd's management in relation to "XY123" is indicative of their deficiencies in this regard and that unless action is taken, the firm's future decision-making capabilities will be severely compromised.

He has therefore requested that Harry prepare a document for him outlining ways in which improvements could be made in this regard. Although not an expert in this area, Harry recalls reading an article recently in Accountancy Ireland which, if he remembers correctly, mentioned advanced financial analysis and benchmarking as techniques that could potentially benefit Smith Ltd in their current predicament. Therefore, as a first step he asks you to log onto the Institute's website and to access the relevant edition of the Journal from their on-line resources, and from there to prepare a report for him which will form the basis for his response to Declan.

> **Task 41: Prepare a report which advises on the use of advanced financial analysis and benchmarking as a means of improving Smith Ltd's management accounting systems and business processes.**

Towards the end of that week, Harry e-mails you and asks you to drop down to his office in the afternoon for a chat. On arriving, Harry firstly informs you that he spoke with Declan Barry earlier that day, and he was very impressed with the report examining possible improvements to Smith Ltd's management accounting systems and business processes. Indeed, Declan has already distributed it to Smith Ltd's senior management team and thus far the vast majority of the feedback received has been very positive.

However, a small number of managers have responded with comments to the effect that although they now realise the importance of having adequate performance measures such as the Balanced Scorecard or Key Performance Indicators in place, they are unsure about the practical issues which are likely to arise when using such measures. As Declan expects the whole area of performance measurement to become increasingly important in the near future, he feels that these comments are justified and therefore warrant his attention.

128 STRATEGIC FINANCE AND MANAGEMENT ACCOUNTING TOOLKIT

Consequently, he has asked Harry to prepare a report for him examining this issue. In light of the sophisticated performance measurement system in operation in Sonner, Saville & Co. Chartered Accountants, Harry feels that this is an assignment that you should be able to complete on your own, and having done so, to send your findings directly to Declan. Harry further informs you that he has already taken the liberty of clearing this with Declan. You're delighted with the additional responsibility and promise Harry to have the report completed by the middle of the following week. Harry agrees with this timeframe and you set off back to your desk to begin this task.

> **Task 42: Prepare a report for Declan which analyses the practical issues which may arise when using performance measures.**

Approximately two weeks later, you meet Harry in the staff canteen and he asks you to meet him in his office after lunch. At this meeting, he tells you that he met Declan at a breakfast briefing organised by the Institute of Directors in Ireland recently, wherein he told him that he was delighted with the report that you had prepared. He also told Harry that at the request of the Board of Directors of Murphy Ltd he gave a presentation at their last meeting on the whole area of performance measurement at Smith Ltd, and much to Harry's delight, he utilised much of the information already provided by Sonner & Saville.

However, at the conclusion of Declan's presentation, there followed what he described as a "robust" discussion amongst the entire Board on this whole area. During this debate, a prominent and highly respected Board member stated that in his opinion any sophisticated performance measurement system should not be viewed in isolation but should instead be linked to strategy. This Director continued by saying that without this connection, there was a distinct possibility that any such performance measurement system would be measuring the wrong items.

As a result of these comments, it was suggested and ultimately agreed upon by the entire Board, that in the context of Smith Ltd, a formal strategy should be devised which would then allow for an agreed upon set of performance measures to be formulated; the achievement of which should result in Smith Ltd achieving their strategic goals.

Declan thought that this was a great idea and has already held a meeting with the senior management team of Smith Ltd to discuss it. At this meeting, there was unanimous agreement on the merits of the proposal and indeed an admission by some senior managers that they have been unclear as to their strategy since the firm was acquired by Murphy Ltd.

On hearing about these developments, Harry suggested to Declan that an external facilitator should be appointed to assist the senior management team at Smith Ltd in determining their future strategy. Declan readily agreed and Harry therefore recommended, Fred Daly, an independent consultant with whom Harry has worked previously. After agreeing to commit to the project, Fred and Declan organised an off-site day for the entire senior management team of Smith Ltd which took place yesterday.

Earlier today, Declan telephoned Harry to tell him that the off-site day was a great success, as the management team collectively agreed on a vision statement and mission statement for Smith Ltd as follows;

Vision Statement
Leadership through World Class Products, Modern Practices and Customer Satisfaction

Mission Statement
To Develop Market Driven Products and to Achieve Customer Satisfaction through Timely Delivery of Quality Products at Competitive Cost by Utilising High Productivity Levels, Trained Human Resources, Team Based and Customer Oriented Work Culture with Continuous Improvement.

As Declan is very eager to maintain the momentum already established, he has asked Harry to assist him in formulating an appropriate strategy and corresponding performance measures for Smith Ltd based upon the outputs from the off-site day. Harry immediately agreed and suggested to Declan that he will draft an initial document which will form the basis for all future discussions between the relevant parties. As this represents a major undertaking, Harry asks you to clear your diary for the next few days and for you to begin the process of drafting a report in response to Declan's requirements. In the meantime, Harry will try and source some additional information from Declan concerning Smith Ltd's future plans. You both agree to meet by the middle of the following week to review progress.

> **Task 43: Based upon the information provided, prepare a report for Harry that identifies an appropriate organisational strategy along with corresponding targets and performance measures for Smith Ltd.**

The following week you meet Harry as agreed to review progress to-date. Harry seems genuinely surprised and delighted by the level of detail contained in your report. Apart from a few minor amendments and some editing, he feels as though the document is of sufficient quality to form the basis for his forthcoming meeting with Declan Barry.

Harry also tells you that he mentioned this task to the firm's Managing Partner, Jeanne Sonner, at their management meeting last week. Jeanne was very complimentary about the work already performed for Murphy Ltd and understands that the feedback from Declan Barry and his colleagues has been very positive. However, having discussed the task at hand, Jeanne suggested that it might be a good idea to contextualise the performance measurement suggestions in terms of how they can assist Smith Ltd in achieving their overall goals.

Harry agrees with Jeanne's assessment and he therefore asks you to draft a memorandum for him to this effect. Once completed, he will include it as a supplement to the strategy, targets and performance measures document which is practically ready to be sent to Declan.

> **Task 44: Prepare a memorandum for Harry that explains how the performance measures developed for Smith Ltd may be used to assist them in achieving their organisational goals.**

Two weeks later, Harry calls you into his office to update you on a meeting he had with Declan earlier that week. According to Harry, Declan was delighted with all of the information and suggestions provided by Sonner & Saville over the previous number of weeks. He also thinks that the senior management team of Smith Ltd are finally beginning to appreciate the critical importance of performance management for the continued success of their business.

Declan also informed Harry of a Board meeting of Murphy Ltd scheduled for later that month, in which the issue of performance management at Smith Ltd is due to be discussed. Although confident as to the progress made in recent times, Declan has heard on the grapevine that some Board members are concerned about the typical conflicts that invariably arise in the context of performance measurement. Therefore, in a pre-emptive effort to respond to these concerns, Declan has requested that Harry prepare a report for him addressing this issue. As Harry is due to attend a family wedding abroad for the remainder of the week, he asks you to draft a report for him, which he will review on his return to work.

> **Task 45: Prepare a report for Harry that demonstrates a detailed understanding of the typical performance measurement conflicts (short-term vs. long-term, financial vs. non-financial and quantified vs. non-quantified).**

Two weeks later, Harry receives a telephone call from Declan, who tells him that the Board of Murphy Ltd is very satisfied with the progress achieved at Smith Ltd in recent times. However, they have recommended that Declan make a presentation to them at the next scheduled meeting outlining Smith Ltd's finalised strategy and corresponding performance measures.

To this end, Declan tells Harry that he has just spent the previous two days attempting to finalise these issues with Smith Ltd's senior management team. During the course of these discussions, Declan became aware that although basic variances were calculated by the Management Accountant in Smith Ltd, the results did not appear to be used to analyse operational performance or for subsequent decision-making purposes. When questioned by Declan as to why this was this case, a number of the managers stated that under the previous ownership regime, any unfavourable variances that occurred were used as a means to apportion blame to specific employees, while any favourable variances were simply ignored.

As a result, managers began to withhold unfavourable information regarding their particular areas, thereby making their own variances appear more favourable than they actually were. Consequently, although variances are still calculated in Smith Ltd, there are serious concerns about the reliability of the results produced, and consequently they are not relied upon for decision-making or performance measurement purposes.

This came as a big surprise to Declan as he's aware that all of Murphy Ltd's manufacturing facilities calculate both basic and advanced variances, and use the information generated for a range of decision-making activities, including performance measurement. Declan quickly realises that he now has a window of opportunity to begin the process of rebuilding senior managers' confidence in the productive use of variance analysis information. Therefore, as a first step he asks Harry to prepare a report for him examining this issue. As Harry knows that you've just completed a major audit of a multi-national firm, he asks you to take the lead in this task.

> **Task 46: Prepare a report for Harry explaining the role of variance analysis in performance measurement.**

The following week, Harry informs you that he spoke with Declan who told him that he was very happy with the report provided, and feels that it will make a big difference in persuading the managers at Smith Ltd of the benefits of using variance analysis for performance measurement purposes. However, having thought about the issues raised at the last meeting, Declan also thinks that if he could provide the management team with a worked example based on real data of the use of advanced variances (i.e. planning and operating variances), then their importance would be re-enforced.

As a result, Declan requests Harry to calculate and analyse a number of advanced variances based on data that he will source from the Production Manager of Smith Ltd. Harry is naturally delighted that Sonner & Saville can be of assistance, and asks you to begin this task once he receives the data from Declan. The following day, you receive an e-mail from Harry containing the following information;

This data relates to the production of a single unit of a component called "EF456". The predetermined standards for the budget period January to March 2008 were set by management in October 2007, and are as follows;

Standard labour hours per unit	1.2
Standard direct labour rate per hour	€/£15.00
Standard price of materials	€/£250 per ounce
Standard usage of materials per unit	1.6 ounces

Research shows that in the quarter ended 31 March 2008 the prevailing market price of materials had been €/£275 per ounce. Since the budget was originally set, the direct labour rate per hour had increased to €/£15.80, reflecting an increase in the national minimum wage as prescribed by Government policy.

During the quarter, modifications to plant and machinery revealed that direct labour hours should be 1.1 per unit, and as a result the standard material usage per unit would fall to 1.5 ounces.

During the quarter ended 31 March 2008 activity and costs revealed the following:

Actual production of "EF456"	10,000 units
Actual materials usage	14,500 ounces
Actual cost of materials used	€/£3,770,000
Actual amount of direct labour used	10,500 hours
Actual cost of direct labour used	€/£168,000

Task 47: Based on the information provided, calculate original variances for; materials price, materials usage, labour rate and labour efficiency. Then, subdivide each original variance into planning and operational variances and analyse the results produced in as much detail as possible.

After confirming your calculations and analysis, Harry compiles a report and sends it to Declan, who immediately contacted the senior management team of Smith Ltd and organised a meeting. At this meeting, Declan provided each of them with copies of your analysis and gave a presentation as to what the results meant and how they could be used for a range of performance measurement purposes. The managers at Smith Ltd were suitably impressed and as a result they have agreed that in the future they would calculate both basic and advanced variances, and would be willing to use the results generated for performance measurement purposes. Declan regards this as great progress, but recognises that care is needed in ensuring that any adverse variances that occur are investigated thoroughly and not simply used as a means to apportion blame to specific employees.

A couple of weeks later, Declan telephones Harry and informs him that in keeping with their expansion plans, Murphy Ltd are seriously considering the purchase of the entire share capital of a Galway-based firm called ABC Ltd, who specialise in the production of a range of components for use in the aeronautical sector. However, one issue that is causing concern relates to the organisational structure of this firm. According to Declan, ABC Ltd is organised on a divisional basis with decisions being taken by managers throughout the organisation, whereas Murphy Ltd has always operated on a centralised basis with all major decisions taken at headquarters by senior management.

It transpires that some of the Board of Directors of Murphy Ltd are of the opinion that should the purchase proceed, then ABC Ltd should be immediately restructured in line with Murphy Ltd, as they believe that to continue with the existing structure would only result in performance measurement difficulties in the future. However, other Board members take the view that as there are many ways of operating a business successfully, then all options should be considered before a final decision is taken.

As a consequence of these differing views, the Board have asked Declan to prepare a report for their next meeting documenting the current structure of ABC Ltd and how performance measurement is conducted therein. Declan tells Harry that after meeting with the Managing Director of ABC Ltd he was informed that the firm is organised on a divisional basis and consists of a number of cost, revenue, profit and investment centres. As Declan is not overly familiar with these structures, he asks Harry to draft a report for him that he can then distribute to the Board at their next meeting. As Harry is aware that you were recently involved in an audit of an indigenous Irish firm which was organised on a divisional basis, he asks you to begin this task, and to e-mail him your findings by the middle of the following week.

PERFORMANCE MEASUREMENT   135

> **Task 48: Draft a report for Harry that distinguishes between the alternative centres for departmental and divisional performance (cost, revenue, profit and investment centres) including how they are assessed and monitored.**

Having completed this task, you meet Harry who tells you that he spoke to Declan the previous afternoon who informed him that he was very happy with the information provided. However, since Harry and Declan's last correspondence, Declan has become aware that some Board members are unsure as to the differences in decision-making approaches adopted in centralised firms like Murphy Ltd as opposed to decentralised firms like ABC Ltd. As a result, Declan has been requested to provide some clarification in this regard, which he duly asked Harry to organise. As Harry was so impressed with your previous task, he asks you to draft a report in response to Declan's request.

> **Task 49: Draft a report for Harry that differentiates between centralised and decentralised decision making approaches.**

A couple of days later you complete your report and e-mail it to Harry, who responds by asking you to drop down to his office that afternoon. At this meeting, Harry is very complementary about your report and feels as though it should significantly clarify a number of the outstanding issues for the Board of Murphy Ltd. However, having previously worked in both centralised and decentralised firms, Harry can appreciate the Board's concerns, and notwithstanding the advice already provided, thinks that they would also appreciate an explanation of the advantages and limitations of divisionalisation. He therefore asks you to begin preparing a memorandum on this issue, and, in the meantime, he will contact Declan and outline his suggestion to him. The following morning, Harry telephones you and tells you that Declan was very much in favour of the additional information, but reminded Harry that as the next scheduled Board meeting of Murphy Ltd is Friday, he will need a completed document by Thursday evening at the very latest to allow for printing, distribution, etc …

Task 50: Draft a memorandum which advises on the advantages and limitations of divisionalisation.

The following Wednesday, you meet Harry as agreed at 2pm in his office. Here, he tells you that according to Declan, the Board of Directors of Murphy Ltd had a very engaging discussion at their meeting last Friday concerning the current decentralised structure of ABC Ltd and the consequent performance measurement implications. Indeed, it appears that a number of Board members were very complimentary about the information provided by Sonner & Saville in this regard, and have asked Declan to pass on their appreciation, which he has duly done.

At the conclusion of the Board meeting, it was unanimously decided that should the purchase of ABC Ltd proceed, then their current decentralised structure should be maintained in the short-term at the very least until a full operational and strategic review is conducted. As the Board are very confident that a deal to acquire ABC Ltd is close to being agreed, they have asked Declan (who has subsequently asked Harry) to prepare a document which compares the various performance measurement techniques currently in use in ABC Ltd. After contacting the Managing Director of ABC Ltd, Declan is informed that as well as using costs and revenue as performance measures, the firm also relies heavily on, profit, Return on Capital Employed (ROCE), Residual Income (RI) and Economic Value Added (EVA).

As Harry is due to attend a two day workshop hosted by the Taxation Institute on "The Harmonisation of European Corporation Tax Rates – Friend or Foe?" he asks you to draft a report for him comparing these measures and to e-mail him your findings. He will then review it on his return from the workshop, before sending it to Declan.

Task 51: Prepare a report for Harry that compares the alternative divisional performance measures, including: profit, ROCE, residual income and economic value added.

Early the following week, Harry telephones you and asks you to meet him in his office in half an hour; at which he informs you that he hasn't reviewed your report yet, but intends to do so later that day. However, he also tells you that while at the workshop, he received an e-mail from

Declan asking him to contact him on his return to work, which he did that morning. From their subsequent conversation, it has emerged that as three of ABC Ltd's divisions (each of which are organised on a geographic basis with each division serving a different European country) utilise a different combination of performance measurement techniques; the Board of Directors of Murphy Ltd have been unable to adequately assess the performance of each division. Consequently, the Chairperson of the Board has made representations to Declan requesting a comparison of the recent performance of these divisions based upon each of the performance measures currently in existence within the firm.

Declan naturally agreed to this request and has asked Harry to perform the analysis once he has sourced the relevant financial information from ABC Ltd. Harry asks you to take the lead in this task once he e-mails you the necessary data. Later that day, you receive the following financials from Harry (all amounts in €/£), while you're also informed that; the French division operates as a profit centre, the other two divisions are treated as investment centres and the cost of capital for ABC Ltd is 7%.

	Divisions		
	France	Germany	Spain
Direct material costs	300,000	400,000	500,000
Direct labour costs	150,000	165,000	180,000
Production overheads	85,000	100,000	130,000
Depreciation	50,000	42,000	60,000
Rent & Rates	35,000	40,000	43,000
Administration costs	65,000	73,000	80,000
R&D costs	200,000	300,000	500,000
Website development costs	55,000	40,000	90,000
Marketing costs	80,000	65,000	100,000
Advertising costs	50,000	60,000	90,000
General expenses	25,000	20,000	15,000
Utilities	10,000	8,000	7,000
Training costs	50,000	75,000	100,000
Bad debts	20,000	15,000	12,000
Insurance	8,000	10,000	11,000
Patent costs	25,000	30,000	40,000
Sales revenue	1,560,000	1,750,000	2,500,000
Capital employed	4,000,000	5,000,000	9,000,000

138 STRATEGIC FINANCE AND MANAGEMENT ACCOUNTING TOOLKIT

> **Task 52: Based on the information provided, calculate the following measures for each division; profit, return on capital employed, residual income and economic value added. Comment upon your results and advise on the most appropriate measure(s) for each division.**

On reviewing your analysis, Harry confirms your findings and sends a report to Declan outlining the recent performance of each division. Later that day, Declan telephones Harry with a few queries. During the course of this conversation, Harry mentions to Declan the potential for dysfunctional consequences as a result of relying solely on short-term measures of performance, including some of those calculated in the report. Declan is intrigued and slightly worried by this proposition and therefore asks Harry to draft a report for him outlining this area in more detail, as he feels that the Board of Directors of Murphy Ltd should be made aware of this issue at their next meeting. Harry subsequently telephones you and asks you to draft a memorandum for him detailing this topic, which will form the basis for his report to Declan.

> **Task 53: Prepare a memorandum that explains the possible dysfunctional consequences of using short term measures of performance.**

The following morning while walking to work, Harry meets Sonner & Saville's, Ethics and Professional Standards Director, Brenda Perry. On hearing about the latest advice offered to Murphy Ltd, Brenda suggests that as there are a range of ethical dilemmas which can potentially occur in the management of divisional performance, these should be considered by Murphy Ltd in accordance with best international practice in this area. Harry thanks Brenda for the advice, and on arriving at his desk, he e-mails you and asks you to draft a report examining this issue as a matter of urgency. In the meantime, he will contact Declan to advise him of the additional information that he will shortly be receiving from Sonner, Saville & Co. Chartered Accountants, which he feels will greatly assist the Board of Directors of Murphy Ltd in deciding whether or not to retain the current divisionalised structure of ABC Ltd should the acquisition be completed.

> **Task 54: Draft a report for Harry that recognises and explains the possible ethical dilemmas which can occur in the management of divisional performance.**

The following week, Declan telephones Harry and thanks him for all of the information provided over the previous few weeks pertaining to divisional performance measures and ethics. Declan also informs Harry that at their most recent Board of Directors meeting, it was collectively decided to lodge a formal offer for the entire share capital of ABC Ltd, which Declan expects to be accepted in due course.

After this decision was taken, one of the firm's senior Executive Directors, Ms. Mary Jones, raised the issue of rising operating costs as a matter requiring their urgent attention. Ms. Jones claimed that because costs at Murphy Ltd for a number of their key components (which are currently sourced externally) had risen significantly over the past number of months, the firm was now less competitive than some of their main competitors and as a result was beginning to lose market share. Ms. Jones further stated that as Smith Ltd currently produces many of the components used by Murphy Ltd, she wondered if some form of transfer pricing agreement between the two firms may represent one means of addressing this issue.

After a brief debate, the Board agreed to discuss the viability of this proposal at their next meeting and therefore asked Declan to prepare some documentation in this regard. As a result, Harry and Declan have agreed to meet the following afternoon in Harry's office to discuss the main issues that are likely to arise. Harry suggests that you should also attend this meeting as he expects you to be involved in this issue going forward. As a basis for the initial discussion with Declan, Harry asks that you prepare a report explaining the fundamentals of transfer pricing.

> **Task 55: Prepare a report that explains the context of transfer pricing. Also, within your report, identify and explain the following issues involved in transfer pricing; aims, approaches and possible conflicts.**

140 STRATEGIC FINANCE AND MANAGEMENT ACCOUNTING TOOLKIT

At the meeting, both Harry and Declan are very impressed by the amount of detail contained in your document, and after a discussion facilitated by Harry, Declan thinks that a transfer pricing agreement between Murphy Ltd and Smith Ltd may indeed be of benefit to both firms and should therefore be investigated further. While Harry agrees with this assessment, he repeatedly stresses to Declan the importance of setting an appropriate transfer price as one of the primary determinants of a successful transfer pricing policy.

Therefore, in order to maintain the momentum, Declan requests that Harry prepare a document for him outlining and advising Murphy Ltd as to the various approaches available in setting transfer prices, which he will then present to the firm's Board of Directors at their next meeting. After Declan leaves, Harry asks you to draft a memorandum for him by the end of the week, which he will then review before submitting to Declan.

> **Task 56: Draft a memorandum that explains and advises Murphy Ltd on the alternative approaches available in setting transfer prices, to include; the cost based methods, the market based method and the negotiated method.**

The following week, Harry telephones you and asks you to meet him in his office in an hour. It transpires that after making a small number of amendments to your memorandum, Harry sent a report to Declan, who subsequently e-mailed it to the Executive Director, Ms. Mary Jones, who had originally raised the issue of transfer pricing at their recent Board meeting.

Having read the report, Mary told Declan that based upon the information provided she felt that the Board of Directors of Murphy Ltd should be able to have an informed debate as to the viability of pursuing a transfer pricing policy with Smith Ltd at their next meeting. However, Mary also felt that the report prepared by Sonner & Saville could be improved upon by outlining potential resolution strategies available to Murphy Ltd in the event of conflicts arising such as failing to agree on an acceptable transfer price with Smith Ltd.

PERFORMANCE MEASUREMENT   141

Having thanked Mary for her input, Declan immediately contacted Harry and relayed the request from Mary. Harry readily agreed to draft a response to Mary's suggestion and to e-mail Declan a revised report by the end of that week. Harry therefore asks you to prepare a document covering this issue which he will then review before sending to Declan. As ever, time is of the essence, so you begin the task that afternoon.

Task 57: Prepare a report for Harry that identifies potential or existing sources of conflict in the area of transfer pricing and which advises on resolution strategies.

TOPIC 4: PERFORMANCE MEASUREMENT

SUGGESTED SOLUTIONS

Solution to Task 36:

Report

To: Harry O'Neill

From: James Crown

Re: A framework for performance measurement

Harry,

I've reviewed the relevant literature and I believe that the following three areas need to be considered within the context of any proposed framework for performance measurement;

1. Controls within an organisation
2. Management accounting control systems
3. Responsibility centres

I will now examine each of these areas in detail;

1. Controls within an organisation

Management exert "control" to ensure that all of the activities performed within a firm contribute to their pre-determined plans and that the firm's objectives are ultimately realised.

"Controls" on the other hand, encompass all of the methods and procedures available to firms to help ensure that their employees are directing their efforts towards achieving the firms' goals and objectives.

2. Management accounting control systems

Management accounting control systems represent the predominant "controls" used within most organisations and consist of a collection of control mechanisms that have primarily an internal focus. Some of the reasons as to why accounting controls predominate are as follows:-

1. All firms need to express and aggregate the results of a wide variety of dissimilar activities using a common measure; and the monetary measure meets this requirement.

2. Profitability and liquidity are essential to the success of all organisations and financial measures relating to these and other areas are closely monitored by stakeholders. It is therefore natural that managers will wish to monitor performance in monetary terms.

3. Financial measures also enable a common decision rule to be applied by all managers when considering alternative courses of action.

4. Measuring results in financial terms enables managers to be given more autonomy. Focusing on the outcomes of managerial actions, summarized in financial terms, gives managers the freedom to take whatever actions they consider to be appropriate so as to achieve the desired results.

5. Outputs expressed in financial terms continue to be effective in uncertain environments even when it is unclear what course of action should be taken. Financial results provide a mechanism to indicate whether the actions benefited the organisation.

Management accounting control systems encompass a range of management accounting techniques (e.g. budgeting, costing, capital investment appraisal, etc …), the use of which provides information to management to support their planning / control and decision-making responsibilities.

Responsibility centre

For the majority of firms, central control is impractical as senior management located at headquarters do not have either the necessary information or time to determine detailed plans for the whole organisation. Therefore, some element of decentralisation is needed for all but the smallest firms. Organisations decentralise by creating responsibility centres, which may be defined as a unit of a firm whereby an individual manager is held responsible for the unit's performance.

There are four main types of responsibility centres as follows;

1. Cost or expense centres
2. Revenue centres
3. Profit centres
4. Investment centres

The creation of responsibility centres is a fundamental part of any management accounting control system. Within each type of centre, various forms of management accounting information are used to determine how the unit and the management of that unit have performed.

Solution to Task 37:

Memorandum

To: Harry O'Neill

From: James Crown

Re: Contingency theory in the context of performance measurement

Harry,

As per your request, I've compiled the following information on contingency theory within the context of formulating a framework for performance measurement;

Contingency Theory

This theory advocates that there is no "one" best design for a management accounting control system that is applicable to all firms in all circumstances. Instead, the most appropriate design for a particular firm will depend upon the situational factors facing the organisation (referred to as the contingent factors).

Examples of contingent factors include the following;

1. **The external environment faced by the organisation:**

   This essentially refers to the amount of environment uncertainty faced by the firm. Examples of uncertainty would include; the degree of unexpected change in customer demand or competitor actions.

   From a management accounting perspective, research (Govindarajan, 1984) has indicated that a rigid budget style of evaluation is more appropriate in firms facing low environmental uncertainty whereas a profit conscious flexible style of evaluation is more appropriate for firms facing high levels of environmental uncertainty.

2. **The type of competitive strategy adopted by a firm:**

   Competitive strategy describes how a firm competes in its chosen industry and attempts to achieve a competitive advantage relative to its competitors. Contingency theory advocates that the management control system in use within a firm must be tailored to support their chosen strategy.

   For example, a low cost competitive strategy requires a greater emphasis on cost controls and frequent and detailed performance reports whereas a differentiation strategy requires less emphasis on tight cost controls and greater reliance on non-financial performance measures.

3. **Technology considerations:**

   Previous research (Chenhall, 2003) focusing on the impact of technology on management accounting control systems has suggested the following;

   (1) The more technologies are characterised by standardised and automated processes the more formal the management accounting controls adopted, e.g. an enhanced reliance on traditional budgeting.

   (2) The more technologies are characterised by high levels of uncertainty, the more informal the management accounting controls adopted resulting in; (i) less reliance on standard operating procedures and accounting performance measures, and (ii) higher participation in budgeting.

4. Business unit, firm and industry variables:

Studies have shown a positive relationship between firm size and management accounting control system sophistication, based mainly on the fact that larger firms have greater access to resources to develop and implement such systems. This fact is demonstrated in studies by Innes & Mitchell, 1995a and Bjornenak, 1997a examining the adoption of Activity Based Costing (ABC).

Similarly, management accounting control systems have been shown to differ by industry type. For example, in a manufacturing environment characterised by a large number of cost centres, a reliance on detailed variance analysis often occurs. In contrast, costs in non-manufacturing industries tend to be discretionary in nature and therefore require other cost control approaches.

Therefore, in advising Murphy Ltd as to their performance measurement requirements, I would suggest that we keep these four factors in mind when offering them advice.

Solution to Task 38:

<u>Report</u>

To: Harry O'Neill

From: James Crown

Re: Viability of "XY123" for the coming financial year

Harry,

I have reviewed the information provided to me, and prior to conducting my analysis, I am making the following assumptions;

In conducting this analysis, I have relied on my understanding that for any item to be considered relevant for decision-making purposes, it must meet the following three criteria;

1. It must be a future item
2. It must be a cash flow

PERFORMANCE MEASUREMENT   147

3. It must differ between alternatives (continue to produce "XY123" v discontinue "XY123")

I have conducted my analysis on the basis that "XY123" would continue to be produced in the coming financial year and that there are only two types of cost – fixed and variable.

On this basis, the following is my analysis as to whether "XY123" should be discontinued;

Sales Revenue   1,200,000

± Relevant Benefits/(Costs)

Direct Materials	(375,000) – only half of the direct materials needed to produce "XY123" need to be purchased as the other half are already in stock (and I'm presuming are already paid for)
	(250,000) – Smith Ltd will not now receive this money from a rival firm, therefore it is the opportunity cost of using the direct materials to produce "XY123" rather than selling them on
Direct Labour (Four full-time employees)	0 – full-time employees' salaries will be paid regardless of the product being discontinued and on that basis, I'm considering them fixed costs
Saving on redundancy	15,385 – (50,000 × 2 × 8/52) – assuming that the product is not discontinued – the firm will not have the pay this amount to the 2 full-time employees as they are not losing their jobs – this is a benefit to Smith Ltd as it represents money that they do not have to spend
Part-time employees	(160,000) – these employees will only be paid if the product continues to be made – I'm assuming that this is the case here

Saving on redundancy	24,615 – (160,000 × 8/52) – as before, because the product is still being made – the firm will not have to pay this redundancy amount to the part-time employees, therefore it represents a saving for Smith Ltd.
Production Overheads	(133,333) – only 2/3 of the production overheads are relevant (i.e. variable) – the other 1/3 will be incurred regardless of whether the product is made or not (i.e. a fixed cost).
Depreciation	0 – only cash flows are relevant to this decision.
Electricity	(56,250) – only 3/4 of this expense is relevant (i.e. variable) – the other 1/4 will be incurred regardless of whether "XY123" is produced or not (i.e. a fixed cost).
Insurance	(25,000) – only 1/2 attributable to the production of "XY123" – the other half will be incurred regardless of whether "XY123" is discontinued.
Rent & Rates	(11,250) – only 1/4 of rent & rates is relevant to this product – the rest will still be incurred even if "XY123" is discontinued.
Supervisor's Salary	0 – the salary expense is a fixed cost and will be incurred as long as "XY123" continues to be produced which is the perspective being adopted here.
Saving on redundancy	12,308 (80,000 × 8/52) – Smith Ltd will not have to pay this amount as the product is not being discontinued – this is a saving for the firm.
Marketing	(40,000) – only 2/3 of this cost if relevant to this product – the other 1/3 will be incurred regardless of whether "XY123" continues to be produced or not.

Administration costs	0 – both of these employees salaries are regarded as fixed and they will be incurred whether "XY123" is produced or not. Therefore they are not relevant here.
	Redundancy payments for these administration staff do not apply as they are not involved in the production of "XY123" – if they were entitled to redundancy payments – then an opportunity benefit would apply here as they will be retained within the firm and therefore Smith Ltd would not be making any such payments to them.
General expenses	(18,000) – only 20% of these apply to "XY123" as the remaining 80% will be incurred even if the product is discontinued.

Revised projected profit 183,475

Based on my analysis, it appears as though "XY123" will actually be profit-making next year to the tune of €/£183,475 and not loss-making as previously suggested. Therefore on this basis, I would recommend that "XY123" should not be discontinued for the coming financial year.

However, in making this decision, it should be borne in mind that ultimately all costs must be covered by the firm, so each of the fixed costs not included in this analysis (e.g. salaries, etc ...) would need to be taken account of in determining Smith Ltd's overall projected profit/loss for the coming year. I would therefore recommend that Smith Ltd undertake such an analysis before making their final decision whether or not to discontinue production of "XY123", as it may be the case that Smith Ltd is budgeted to be loss-making for the coming year.

150 STRATEGIC FINANCE AND MANAGEMENT ACCOUNTING TOOLKIT

Solution to Task 39:

Memorandum

To: Harry O'Neill

From: James Crown

Re: "Other" considerations in regard to the viability of "XY123"

Harry,

This memorandum outlines some of the issues that Declan ought to consider prior to making his final decision as to the continued viability of "XY123" under the following three headings, each of which I will subsequently examine in more detail;

1. Non-financial
2. Environmental
3. Ethical

1. Non-financial issues

1. Declan should firstly consider the accuracy of the financial projections provided. Specifically, he needs to determine how the figures were calculated, and what, if any, assumptions were made, as it may be the case that some or all of these were unrealistic. If this is the case, then he will need to re-do the financial analysis based upon more realistic assumptions.

2. He also needs to consider the reaction of Smith Ltd's staff if "XY123" is discontinued and some of the firms employees are subsequently made redundant. If this occurs, it may make other employees uneasy concerning their own positions within the firm, and they may begin to seek employment opportunities elsewhere. Therefore, the remaining staff will need to be re-assured by management concerning their own positions.

3. Declan would need to ensure that in the event of a decision been made regarding redundancies, that any trade unions recognised by the firm are involved in the process of agreeing on an acceptable redundancy package (perhaps exceeding the minimum prescribed under EU labour laws) and that re-training is offered to all employees. Otherwise industrial unrest

may ensue which could disrupt production and result in a delay in customers receiving their orders.

2. Environmental issues

1. Smith Ltd would need to consider their competitors reaction if they were to discontinue production of "XY123", as by doing so they are effectively allowing their rivals to dominate the market for this particular product. Declan and his senior management team need to decide whether they are prepared to allow this to occur.

2. Similarly, Declan needs to consider their customers reaction if this product is discontinued. As some customers like to purchase a suite of products from the same firm, this may result in some customers switching to rival firms for other products also, which may result in Smith Ltd losing market share.

3. Management at Smith Ltd would need to consider their shareholders reaction if they were to cease production of "XY123". Some shareholders may perceive this as the wrong decision and as a result may sell their shares in the firm, which could cause funding and even publicity difficulties for the firm in the future.

3. Ethical dimensions

1. From a staff perspective, discontinuing this product may result in redundancies for some staff who may have worked for the firm for a long period of time. If this is the case, then the firm needs to ensure that these employees are adequately compensated for their loss of employment. This may mean that the firm pays these employees more than they are legally entitled to.

2. From a customer perspective, discontinuing "XY123" may place some customers in a difficult position re their own competitiveness. As some of these customers are likely to be loyal customers who have traded with Smith Ltd for many years, and may indeed also purchase other products from them; this process would need to be managed carefully and adequate notice given to these customers to ensure that their goodwill is not jeopardised.

152 STRATEGIC FINANCE AND MANAGEMENT ACCOUNTING TOOLKIT

3. By discontinuing "XY123", it may mean that Smith Ltd no longer needs to employ certain suppliers who contributed to the production of this product. If this is the case, then these firms would need to be contacted at the earliest possible opportunity and informed of the decision, so that they can try and source other business elsewhere. Failure to do so may result in some of these firms having to make some of their employees redundant in the short-term at least.

Solution to Task 40:

Report

To: Harry O'Neill

From: James Crown

Re: New developments in management accounting

Harry,

I've done some research on some of the new developments in management accounting from a performance management perspective, and I will now outline what I have found in relation to the following three areas:

1. Critical Success Factors (CSFs)
2. Key Performance Indicators (KPIs)
3. Balanced Scorecard (BSC)

1. Critical Success Factors (CSFs)

Critical success factors represent those areas that a firm must perform well in for them to be considered successful. These areas will have been identified by senior management as critical to the continued success of their firm going forward and will invariably change in tandem with the firm's trading circumstances. Examples of CSFs might include; sales volume, market share, number of product returns, etc … In line with contingency theory, the CSFs selected by every firm will differ according to the individual circumstances that each faces.

2. Key Performance Indicators (KPIs)

Key performance indicators are linked to the CSFs outlined above, in that for a firm's CSFs to be achieved, they will need to be formulated in terms of related performance measures or indicators. Performance measures are direct measures such as measuring employee satisfaction by way of an annual survey. Alternatively, performance indicators require the use of proxy measures. For example, a firm attempting to determine employee satisfaction may regard the number of employees who leave their firm voluntarily each year as indicative of this issue. Examples of KPIs might include; number of patents registered, number of new products launched, number of new customers, etc ...

3. Balanced Scorecard (BSC)

The Balanced Scorecard (BSC) was developed by Robert Kaplan and David Norton in response to managers' calls for a broader range of performance measurement items than purely traditional financial measures (e.g. profit, turnover, etc ...). The BSC is therefore composed of the following four perspectives, the ultimate aim of which is to allow management a fast but comprehensive view as to how their business is performing; financial, customer, internal business and learning and growth.

Each perspective attempts to allow firms to answer a different question as follows:

1. Financial perspective – how do we look to our shareholders?
2. Customer perspective – How do our customers see us?
3. Internal business perspective – What must we excel at internally?
4. Learning and growth perspective – Can we continue to improve and create value?

The BSC is "balanced" in three ways; (1) it includes internal and external measures, (2) it uses financial and non-financial measures and (3) the four perspectives are balanced in respect of time in so far as they incorporate the past (financial perspective), the present (customer and internal business perspectives) and the future (learning and growth perspective).

From an operational perspective, each firm (entity) is advised to formulate a number of goals for each perspective, which is then augmented by the formulation of a number of performance measures (indicators). As all of these items should be linked to the firm's overall strategy; the belief is that by achieving the performance measures, a firm will achieve its goals and by doing so will also achieve their strategy.

However, as with all performance measurement frameworks there are a number of criticisms that ought to be considered before a decision is taken to implement it. A number of the more prominent ones associated with the BSC are as follows;

1. It's difficult (if not impossible) to conduct a cost-benefit analysis in respect of the BSC and, as a result, firms are investing substantial amounts of time and money for often unquantifiable results. One of the major issues here is that many of the benefits of the Balanced Scorecard are intangible, e.g. improved (streamlined) processes. Therefore it's very difficult for firms to determine whether the benefits of implementing and maintaining the BSC exceed the cost.

2. Some have argued that the implementation of the BSC in some firms has only resulted in information overload for some managers. The argument here is that as some managers were already overburdened by financial metrics, adding another three perspectives into the mix has only made the problem even worse.

3. It has been suggested that managers may select performance measures for inclusion in their BSC with which they are most familiar rather than those that will lead to enhanced financial success. Similarly, managers may select performance measures that highlight strengths rather than areas that need improvement in an effort to enhance the perception of their own performance.

PERFORMANCE MEASUREMENT   155

Solution to Task 47:

Report

To: Harry O'Neill

From: James Crown

Re: The use of advanced financial analysis and benchmarking to improve Smith Ltd's management accounting systems and business processes

Harry,

Based upon the research that I've undertaken, I believe that advanced financial analysis and benchmarking could potentially be used by Smith Ltd to improve both their management accounting systems and business processes for the following reasons:

Advanced financial analysis

From my analysis it would appear that Smith Ltd employs a standard set of management accounting systems and business processes in conducting their daily tasks. However, the use of more advanced techniques may allow them to enhance their performance in a number of key areas.

For example, in terms of cost management, Smith Ltd could implement some of the following modern approaches;

1. Target Costing

Target costing is beneficial when a firm knows (or has a good idea) what sales price should be charged for a proposed new product, but is unsure about how to develop a product which can be marketed profitably at the desired price. The use of target costing therefore allows a firm to determine the maximum allowable cost for a new product and then to develop a prototype that can be profitably made for the maximum target cost figure. Essentially, the target cost is set first and then the product is designed so that the target cost is attained. Once the firm decides on the overall target cost, it is then broken down into target costs for each function (department), who must ensure that they keep their own costs within target for

156 STRATEGIC FINANCE AND MANAGEMENT ACCOUNTING TOOLKIT

the process to succeed. The main reason for implementing target costing is that as the majority of the cost of a product is incurred in the design stage, once a product is designed and has gone into production, not much can be done to significantly reduce its cost.

2. Life Cycle Costing

Life cycle costing estimates and gathers costs over a product's entire life-cycle (i.e. a number of years) thereby allowing management to determine whether the profits earned during a product's manufacturing phase will cover the costs incurred during the pre and post manufacturing phases. The primary benefit of this approach is that it allows management to understand the cost consequences of developing and manufacturing a product, whilst also identifying areas where cost reduction efforts are likely to be successful.

3. Activity Based Costing (ABC)/Activity Based Management (ABM)

With overhead costs increasing rapidly for many firms, there has been a growing feeling that the traditional approach to overhead absorption/ allocation did not reflect increasingly complex organisational processes, i.e. allocating overheads to products / services on the basis of labour hours was inappropriate to an operating environment increasingly character-ised by high levels of automation. Therefore, ABC aims to identify the activities (e.g. number of products produced, number of machine set-ups, etc) that cause overhead costs to be incurred and to apportion these costs to products / services on that basis. As ABC necessitates that a number of cost drivers are identified, it is generally regarded as a more accurate cost allocation basis than traditional absorption costing, and as a result it should lead to enhanced decision-making on the part of management.

For the use of ABC to be successful within any organisation, a number of conditions need to be met as outlined below:

1. Production overheads are high relative to direct costs.
2. Great diversity in product range.
3. Considerable diversity of overhead resource input to products.
4. Consumption of overheads not particularly driven by volume but by activities.

Based on the ABC data, firms have a number of options available to them, which are collectively referred to as Activity Based Management (ABM). Some of these are as follows:

1. Re-price, redesign or eliminate products
2. Perform customer profitability analysis
3. Improve processes and operations strategy

In summary, the merits/criticisms of ABC / ABM include;

Merits

1. Focuses attention on the nature of cost behaviour and attempts to provide meaningful product costs.

2. Allows firms to assess product and customer profitability realistically.
3. Can give valuable insights into product design, mix, processing methods and pricing.

Criticisms

1. Should not be introduced unless it provides extra information to management for planning/control purposes.
2. Claimed to provide more accurate product cost information:
   - Only if relevant cost drivers have been identified;
   - May result in significant systems and implementation costs.
3. Benefits may be more meaningful to larger firms.

In terms of improving Smith Ltd's business processes, I would suggest the use of Business Process Re-engineering (BPR) for the following reasons:

4. Business Process Re-engineering (BPR)

This approach involves examining a firm's business processes (e.g. materials handling) and making substantial changes to how they currently operate by redesigning how work within an organisation is performed. The aim of BPR is to improve a firm's key processes by focusing on factors such as; simplification, cost reduction, improved quality, etc … BPR has become synonymous with radical changes to current processes in an attempt to make them more efficient.

In terms of planning and controlling stocks and the supply chain in general, Smith Ltd could consider using some of the following advanced management accounting techniques:

5. Just In Time (JIT)

The implementation of a JIT system requires the purchase of materials and the production of goods only as needed. This should result in stock being reduced to a minimum (or, in some instances, zero), which in turn should reduce ordering and warehousing costs. The primary benefits of implementing the JIT approach include the following:

1. Working capital is bolstered therefore less money is tied up in stock.
2. Areas used to store stock can now be used for other purposes.
3. Throughput time is reduced resulting in a quicker response to customers.
4. Defect rates are reduced which should result in enhanced customer satisfaction.

6. Backflush Costing

This is a simplified costing system that aims to eliminate detailed accounting transactions, and is generally applied when a JIT approach is adopted. Instead of tracking the movement of materials through the production process, a backflush costing system focuses first on the output of the firm and then works backwards when allocating cost between:

1. Cost of goods sold; and
2. Stock.

Therefore, there is no separate accounting for work-in-progress (WIP), which is in contrast to a conventional system which tracks costs in tandem with the movement of goods from direct materials, through WIP to finished goods.

7. Materials Requirements Planning (MRP I)

MRP I is a computerised approach for coordinating the planning of the purchase of materials and production. Within MRP I materials are only ordered that are required to maintain the manufacturing flow. MRP I firstly determines the quantity and timing of finished goods demanded. Using this information, it helps to determine the requirements for raw materials components and sub-assemblies at each of the prior stages of production. MRP I produces a time-phased schedule of order releases of lower-level items for purchasing and manufacturing, and takes stock and expected lead times, etc. into account.

8. Manufacturing Resources Planning (MRP II)

MRP I was later extended to provide an integrated planning approach to the management of all manufacturing resources and has become known as MRP II. In particular, it focuses on machine capacity planning and labour scheduling in addition to materials planning.

9. Enterprise Resource Planning (ERP) systems

ERP systems refer to a set of integrated software application modules that aim to control all of the information flows within a firm and cover most business functions (including accounting). All modules are fully integrated, so users can access real-time information on all aspects of the business. Data is entered only – typically where the data originates. Potentially ERP systems can have a major impact on the work performed by management accountants, such as reducing routine information gathering and processing.

Finally, the last section of this report examines how the use of benchmarking may represent one means by which Smith Ltd could improve both their management accounting systems and business processes.

Benchmarking

Benchmarking would involve Smith Ltd performing an internal audit of their current management accounting systems and business processes and comparing what they have to those of their competitors. By performing this task, Smith Ltd can quickly identify those areas where they are in a better position than their rivals, and those areas where they are deficient in comparison with their competitors. By accumulating this information, Smith Ltd can then take steps to either increase the gap between themselves and their rivals (in the case of systems or processes where they are superior to their rivals), or in the case of deficient areas reduce the gap.

In terms of any benchmarking exercise that Smith Ltd may engage in, it has been argued that the process of benchmarking should be conducted in comparison to world-class firms, who do not necessarily have to be operating in the same industry. Indeed, it may be advantageous to study firms from other sectors who have developed new management accounting systems and / or business processes which could potentially be used by Smith Ltd, thus giving them a competitive advantage over their rivals in the same sector who are unaware of these particular developments.

Solution to Task 42:

Report

To: Declan Barry

From: James Crown

Cc: Harry O'Neill

Re: The practical issues which may arise when using performance measures.

Declan,

Based on my analysis, I have outlined some of the practical issues which may arise when using performance measures and which will need to be considered by Smith Ltd;

1. What measures to include?

There may be some debate amongst management as to what measures should be included in a firm's performance measurement system. The basic premise for the inclusion of any measure is that it should be representative of the firm's strategy, and if not, then it should not be included unless there is a valid reason for doing so. A decision also needs to be taken as to who will actually select the measures to be included, as a conflict of interest may ensue if individual employees are involved in selecting the measures upon which they are to be ultimately evaluated.

2. How often items are to be measured?

Each firm will need to decide how often they wish to measure each item. For example, are customer satisfaction surveys to be undertaken every three months or once a year? Items that are measured too frequently may become a chore for those involved and may soon lose their appeal. Alternatively, items that are not measured frequently enough may result in the firm missing out on potential opportunities to respond quickly to market changes.

3. Who is responsible for collecting the necessary data?

As a number of departments/units within a firm may feel that the collection of data relating to a certain performance measure is their responsibility, each firm will need to decide from the outset who exactly is responsible for collecting certain data. Failure to do so may result in a number of employees collecting similar data which is both a waste of time and money from the firm's perspective.

4. Who should have access to the results?

As above, the firm will need to decide early on, who is to be allowed have access to the results. Certain items may be regarded as commercially sensitive and may therefore be restricted to senior management only. Controls will need to be designed and implemented (e.g. passwords, etc …) to ensure that unauthorised access to performance measurement data does not occur.

5. Will the results be linked to employee evaluations?

Many firms link the results from their performance measurement system to their employees' performance evaluations. If this is to be the case in Smith Ltd, then their employees need to be made aware of this from the outset. If this is to be the model adopted, then any trade unions recognised by the firm will also need to be involved to ensure that all employees concerns are adequately addressed.

6. Senior management commitment?

Without senior management commitment to the use of performance measures, the probability is that their use will not be successful in any organisation. Therefore, top management needs to be seen to be supporting the introduction of performance measures from their initial consideration through to their implementation.

Please contact me if you require any further information or clarification.

Yours truly,
James Crown
Trainee Chartered Accountant
Sonner, Saville & Co. Chartered Accountants

Solution to Task 43:

Report

To: Harry O'Neill

From: James Crown

Re: Strategy, targets and performance measures for Smith Ltd

Harry,

Having reviewed the vision statement and mission statement agreed by the management of Smith Ltd at their off-site day, along with my own knowledge of the organisation, this report outlines; a strategy, targets and corresponding performance measures which may be used by the firm in determining their future competitive position.

Strategy

I would recommend that Smith Ltd continue to focus their attention on the automotive sector and within this to pursue a product differentiation strategy based on quality.

Targets

In keeping with the strategy outlined above (and the vision and mission statements), I believe that Smith Ltd should focus on the following four areas:

1. Customer satisfaction.
2. Continual improvements in product quality.
3. Human resources.
4. Product innovation.

Performance Measures

To ensure that Smith Ltd achieves their four pre-determined targets, I am recommending that they develop the following performance measures for each;

1. Customer satisfaction

Number of repeat orders
% of market share
Customer satisfaction

2. Continual improvements in product quality

Number of defects
Production yield
% of products returned

3. Human resources

Average number of training days per employee
Number of graduates employed
Number of employees who voluntarily left the firm in the past year

4. Product innovation

% of revenue from new products
Expenditure on R&D
Number of new patents registered

164 STRATEGIC FINANCE AND MANAGEMENT ACCOUNTING TOOLKIT

Solution to Task 44:

Memorandum

To: Harry O'Neill

From: James Crown

Re: A contextualisation of the performance measures developed for Smith Ltd

Harry,

This memorandum outlines how the performance measures developed for Smith Ltd can assist them in achieving their targets, which in-turn should result in them achieving their strategy.

The strategy recommended for Smith Ltd is that they continue to target the automotive sector as this is where they have built up significant expertise and relationships over the past number of years. In terms of the strategy that they adopt within this sector, I have suggested a product differentiation strategy based on product quality as the focus of their attention, as this is in-keeping with their vision and mission statements. In my opinion, Smith Ltd should not pursue a cost leadership position as to do so would indicate to their customers and other stakeholders, that low cost and not product quality is their over-riding concern.

Based on the above, I have outlined a series of targets that Smith Ltd needs to focus on to ensure that their strategy is achieved. Specifically, these relate to; customer satisfaction, continual improvements in product quality, human resources and product quality. By concentrating on these specific areas, Smith Ltd will ensure that it maintains a focus on those areas that are of paramount importance to the achievement of their strategy.

To ensure that this is the case, I have devised a series of performance measures for each of their four targets which I will now outline.

1. Customer satisfaction

1. Number of repeat orders – this measures the extent to which customers purchase goods from Smith Ltd on an on-going basis. A fall in this measure

would indicate a decline in sales, and would need to be investigated. An increase in this measure would suggest that customers are happy with the levels of service provided and as long as this can be maintained and enhanced where possible, then I would expect this measure to increase in the future.

2. % of market share – this measures how much of the overall amount of electrical components sold in the automotive sector is done by Smith Ltd. An increase in this measure would suggest that the firm has acquired market share from their competitors while a reduction would suggest that their rivals have secured some of Smith Ltd's market share. As a decline in market share is often viewed as more critical than a decline in sales, this is an important performance measure for the firm's management to review on an on-going basis.

3. Customer satisfaction survey – this will measure the satisfaction of Smith Ltd's customers in relation to for example; the levels of service provided, price paid, etc. Any increase in this measure is to be welcomed, while any reduction would need to be researched and efforts taken to redress any issues that are identified as soon as possible.

2. Continual improvements in product quality

1. Number of defects – this in an internal control measure to determine how many products were not manufactured correctly at the first attempt. As with the other performance measures, Smith Ltd would need to set a target for this measure that they don't wish to exceed. If they do surpass this target, research would need to be undertaken to find out why, and immediate action taken to remedy the situation.

2. Production yield – this measures how much output is generated for a given level of inputs. This will measure how efficient Smith Ltd is in producing their required levels of output at the requisite quality standard. As before, any variation from their predetermined production standards would need to be investigated to ensure that any adverse variances are not allowed to persist.

3. % of products returned – this is an external measure that seeks to discover if customers are satisfied with the products produced by Smith Ltd. All firms will have a certain amount of returns each period, but if the amount exceeds their target, then they will need to find out why, as to

allow this situation to continue may ultimately result in a loss of custom to some of their competitors.

3. Human resources

1. Average number of training days per employee – this will measure the firm's commitment to ensuring that their employees' skills are kept as up-to-date as possible. For this measure to be viable, Smith Ltd will need to provide relevant training courses while employees need to be encouraged to partake in them.

2. Number of graduates employed – if Smith Ltd is serious about product innovation, then it should follow that they employ a significant number of graduates each year. An increase in this measure would suggest that graduates regard Smith Ltd as an excellent place to work and would re-enforce their reputation in the marketplace. A reduction would indicate that graduates feel that they would be better off elsewhere and may indicate an issue that Smith Ltd needs to address.

3. Number of employees who voluntarily left the firm in the past year – within any firm a certain number of employees resign each year. However, if this measure becomes too big it may indicate that employees feel that Smith Ltd is not offering them the best possible opportunities in comparison to their competitors. This may result in a problem for Smith Ltd if too much of their Intellectual Capital leaves over a short period of time.

4. Product innovation

1. % of revenue from new products – this measure will allow Smith Ltd to determine if their newly released products are selling in the marketplace as they would have expected. If not, they may need to review some of their offerings (e.g. sales price, functionality, etc …), and in the worst case scenario perhaps even withdraw them from sale.

2. Expenditure on R&D – as all firms need to have a number of new products in the pipeline, this measure will allow them to determine whether or not they are spending enough money on developing new products. A fall in this measure may have some short-term benefits in terms of increased profitability, but in the medium to long-term, it may allow their

competitors to bring new products to market at a faster rate which may reduce their overall market share.

3. Number of new patents registered – this measure will allow Smith Ltd to see if the money spent on R&D is generating an acceptable return for them, as if the number of new patents registered falls, it may mean that the firm's R&D process is not delivering the number of new products that it should. By not registering new patents on an on-going basis, Smith Ltd may lose out to their competitors who are actively doing so.

Solution to Task 45:

Report

To: Harry O'Neill

From: James Crown

Re: Typical conflicts in the area of performance measurement

Harry,

As you requested, my report will address the following three typical conflicts that can occur in the area of performance measurement;

1. Short term vs. long term
2. Financial vs. non-financial
3. Quantified vs. non-quantified

1. Short term vs. long term

Any performance measurement system should include both short and long term measures of performance to reflect the fact that firms also have both short and long term objectives. The potential dilemma here is that some managers may focus their attention on achieving the short-term measures of performance to the detriment of the firm's longer term objectives. This may be the case where managers are rewarded on the basis of achieving a short-term measure, for example, a pre-determined profit figure. However, the achievement of this profit target may have been done so at the expense of some of the firm's longer term targets, such as increased market share. Therefore, to overcome this potential issue, managers should be rewarded on the basis of a combination of both short and long term measures of performance.

2. Financial vs. non-financial
In this instance, managers may focus solely on achieving their firm's financial targets, and ignore the range of non-financial factors which are also increasingly important for both firms and their stakeholders. For example, a manager of a profit centre may concentrate on achieving his/her profit target whilst failing to gauge whether his/her customers are satisfied with the levels of service provided. If this latter situation is negative and not addressed, then their customers may begin to shop elsewhere, which will invariably result in reduced future profits. Consequently, a combination of both financial and non-financial measures of performance should be included in any performance measurement system.

3. Quantified vs. non-quantified
Quantified information may be relatively easy for managers to access and analyse for performance measurement purposes (e.g. number of new products launched in the last year). However, non-quantified information (e.g. customer satisfaction in relation to new products launched in the last year) may be equally important for a manager to determine even though this information may be more difficult to acquire. The challenge therefore for management is to ensure that they consider both quantified and non-quantified information when making performance measurement decisions.

Solution to Task 46:

<u>Report</u>

To: Harry O'Neill

From: James Crown

Re: The role of variance analysis in performance measurement

Harry,

The use of variance analysis information is important as it allows firms to determine both their effectiveness (i.e. the degree to which an objective, goal or target was met) and/or their efficiency (i.e. the degree to which inputs are used in relation to a given level of outputs).

Once appropriate variances (e.g. sales, materials, labour, etc.) have been calculated, a firm can easily identify those areas that are performing better than expected and those that are not (i.e. above or below pre-determined budgetary targets). Within these areas (both favourable and unfavourable), different employees may be responsible for different sections, e.g. the purchasing manager or the production manager. On the basis of the variance analysis information, the appropriate employee can be identified and action can be taken to either build upon the favourable result, or corrective action taken in relation to the unfavourable result.

A big danger with the use of variance analysis for performance measurement purposes is if the results are used to apportion blame if an employee fails to reach their predetermined targets. If this is the case, then the reasons for the adverse (unfavourable) variance(s) should be investigated as it may be the case that factors outside the employees control are partially or totally responsible for the results achieved (e.g. a global health scare for a particular food product).

Firms who use variance analysis to apportion blame, often find that employees may resort to withholding or misstating valuable information in an attempt to ensure that blame for the poor result will not be totally directed at them.

Firms should always keep in mind when analysing the results from variance analysis that performance in one area of operations is likely to impact on other areas. For example, a purchasing manager who sources cheap but inferior quality raw materials will probably attain a favourable material price variance, whereas for the production manager, the result is likely to be an unfavourable material usage variance.

As a consequence of the linkages between variances, one should not jump to conclusions regarding the results attained. By themselves variances simply raise questions and provide clues as to the causes of performance. However, in the vast majority of cases, further analysis is then needed to determine what exactly has occurred.

Solution to Task 47:

Calculation of Variances

To: Harry O'Neill

From: James Crown

Re: Calculation of variances

Harry,

As per your request, I have calculated the four original variances as follows (please note that F = Favourable and U = Unfavourable);

1. **Materials price variance**
   (SP − AP) × AQ
   (€/£250 − €/£260*) × 14,500 =   €/£145,000 U
   *€/£260 = €/£3,770,000/14,500

2. **Materials usage variance**
   (SQ − AQ) × SP
   ((10,000 × 1.6) − 14,500) × €250
   (16,000 − 14,500) × €/£250 =   €/£375,000 F **€/£230,000 F**

PERFORMANCE MEASUREMENT 171

3. Labour rate variance
$(SR - AR) \times AH$
$(€/£15 - €16^*) \times 10,500 = \qquad €/£10,500$ U
$^*€/£16 = €168,000/10,500$

4. Labour efficiency variance
$(SH - AH) \times SR$
$((10,000 \times 1.2) - 10,500) \times €15$
$(12,000 - 10,500) \times €/£15 = \qquad €/£22,500$ F   **€/£12,000 F**

Analysis

The results suggest that Smith Ltd paid more for their materials during the quarter than they had originally budgeted for (€/£260 vs. €/£250). However, they used fewer materials to produce the desired level of output than they had planned to (14,500 ounces vs. 16,000 ounces).

As regards labour, the results indicate that Smith Ltd paid their employees more per hour than they expected during the quarter (€/£16 vs. €/£15), but on the other hand, their employees were more efficient in terms of the time taken to produce the actual level of output (10,500 hours vs. 12,000 hours).

These "original" variances can be further broken down into their planning and operational components. Please note that the analysis provided here makes use of ex post and ex ante formulae as follows;

Ex Post (XP) – revised budget/standard

Ex Ante (XA) – original budget/standard

The main benefit of planning and operational variances is that it allows management to separate out which variances are due to planning errors (regarded as uncontrollable) and which are due to operational variances (are controllable and will need to be investigated). I will now present the results of my analysis.

STRATEGIC FINANCE AND MANAGEMENT ACCOUNTING TOOLKIT

Direct materials – planning variances (bringing the original standards up-to-date)

5. **Price**
   (XPSP – XASP) × XPSQ
   (€/£275 – €/£250) × 15,000* =   €/£375,000 U
   *15,000 = 10,000 × 1.5

6. **Usage**
   (XPSQ – XASQ) × XASP
   (15,000 – 16,000*) × €/£250 =   €/£250,000 F
   *16,000 = 10,000 × 1.6

Direct materials - operational variances (extent to which the updated standards have been met)

7. **Price**
   (AP – XPSP) × AQ
   (€/£260 – €/£275) × 14,500 =   €/£217,500 F

8. **Usage**
   (AQ – XPSQ) × XPSP
   (14,500 – 15,000) × €/£275 =   €/£137,500 F **€/£230,000 F**

Analysis:
1. Price
The planning variance is unfavourable (€/£375,000) as it reveals that the market price for raw materials increased from €250 per ounce to €/£275 per ounce during the quarter. However, the operational variance is favourable as the actual price paid for raw materials was €260 per ounce, which resulted in a favourable variance of €/£217,500.

2. Usage
Both of the usage variances are favourable. The planning variance of €/£250,000 indicates that due to the modifications to the firm's plant and machinery, it is now only taking 1.5 ounces of materials to make each product as opposed to 1.6 ounces previously. The favourable opera-

PERFORMANCE MEASUREMENT   173

tional variance of €/£137,500 reveals that the firm is efficient in terms of materials usage, as they only used 14,500 ounces of materials to produce 10,000 units rather than the anticipated 15,000 ounces.

Direct labour – planning variances (bringing the original standards up-to-date)

9. **Rate**
   (XPSR – XASR) × XPSH
   (€/£15.80 – €/£15.00) × 11,000* = €/£8,800 U
   *11,000 = 10,000 × 1.1

10. **Efficiency**
    (XPSH – XASH) × XASR
    (11,000 – 12,000*) × €/£15.00 =   €/£15,000 F
    *12,000 = 10,000 × 1.2

Direct labour - operational variances (extent to which the updated standards have been met)

11. **Rate**
    (AR – XPSR) × AH
    (€/£16.00 – €/£15.80) × 10,500 = €/£2,100 U

12. **Efficiency**
    (AH – XPSH) × XPSR
    (10,500 – 11,000) × €/£15.80 =   €/£7,900 F   **€/£12,000 F**

Analysis:
1. Rate
Both the planning and operational variances are unfavourable. The planning variance is unfavourable as it takes into account the increase in the national minimum wage from €/£15 per hour to €/£15.80 per hour. However, in reality the firm paid their employees €/£16 per hour, hence why the operational variance is unfavourable.

2. Efficiency

Both of the efficiency variances are favourable. The planning variance (€/£15,000) is due to the fact that because of the modifications to plant and machinery, it now takes 1.1 direct labour hours to make each product as opposed to 1.2 direct labour hours previously. However, even though it should have taken 11,000 direct labour hours to produce 10,000 units of "EF456", it only took the firm 10,500 hours, hence why they have a favourable efficiency variance.

Solution to Task 48:

Report

To: Harry O'Neill

From: James Crown

Re: Alternative centres for departmental and divisional performance

Harry,

As per your instructions, I have examined each of the four following divisional structures, all of which are in use in ABC Ltd.

1. Cost centre
2. Revenue centre
3. Profit centre
4. Investment centre

I will now outline each of these in detail, including how they are assessed and monitored.

1. Cost centre

This refers to an organisational structure wherein managers are only responsible for the costs under their control. Examples of cost centres may include the following departments (divisions); human resources, accounting, marketing, information technology, etc. Although cost centre managers are not directly accountable for sales revenue, they can affect the amount of sales revenue generated if quality standards are not maintained or if output is not produced to schedule. In these structures, managers are given a budget for the coming financial year and are expected to keep within it. At the end of the year, the management of each cost centre is then evaluated on this basis, i.e. how much they spent in comparison to their budget allocation.

2. Revenue centre

Within a revenue centre, managers are responsible for maximising sales revenue. The sales division (department) is the primary example of such an entity. Managers in a revenue centre are given a budget at the start of the year as to the amount of sales revenue that they are expected to generate. At the end of the year, they are evaluated on the basis of whether or not they have met this target. A possible danger with this form of entity is that it may encourage managers to concentrate on maximising sales revenues at the expense of profitability. This can occur when all sales are not equally profitable and managers can achieve higher sales revenues by promoting low-profit products. Some revenue centre managers may be held accountable for selling expenses, but are not accountable for the cost of goods sold and services that they sell.

3. Profit centre

In a profit centre, a manager has responsibility for both of the components comprising profit, i.e. cost and revenue. S/he has the authority to make decisions regarding these components in the expectation that they will increase their division's overall profit (e.g. what price to charge and which markets to sell in). As before, managers operating within this form of structure are given a profit target at the beginning of the year, and it is on this basis that they are subsequently evaluated.

4. Investment centre

In an investment centre, managers have responsibility for cost, revenue, working capital and capital investment decisions up to a certain predefined threshold determined by headquarters. Investment centres represent the highest level of managerial responsibility and managers are generally evaluated on the basis of return on investment or economic value added, in recognition of the significant levels of authority vested in them.

176 STRATEGIC FINANCE AND MANAGEMENT ACCOUNTING TOOLKIT

Investment centres can include the firm as a whole, operating subsidiaries, operating groups and divisions.

Solution to Task 49:

Report

To: Harry O'Neill

From: James Crown

Re: Differences between centralised and decentralised decision making approaches

Harry,

This report outlines the major differences between centralised and decentralised decision making approaches.

Centralised decision-making

In a centralised firm like Murphy Ltd, all major decisions are taken by senior management located centrally (i.e. at the firm's headquarters). Consequently, local managers based in each region or division do not have decision-making powers themselves, but rather implement the decisions already taken by central management. As a result of this concentration of decision-making power at the centre of the firm; centralised decision-making is generally regarded as a very controlled operating environment.

However, it has also been argued that as a result of centralised decision-making, control and co-ordination is easier to maintain along with the fact that policies and procedures can be easily standardised firm-wide. Furthermore, it has also been suggested that because senior management based centrally are making all of the key decisions, they can take a wide view of any issues that arise and can therefore keep a balance between all of their departments/divisions. Finally, as these decision-makers are both highly skilled and experienced, it has been argued that the quality of their decision-making maybe higher than those taken locally.

PERFORMANCE MEASUREMENT 177

Decentralised decision-making

Decentralised decision-making refers to the situation in which local level managers in each division/region/department are permitted to take decisions up to a certain threshold without referring to central management for approval. The type of decision that each manager is allowed to take depends on the type of divisional entity involved. For example, a manager in a profit centre structure should be allowed to make decisions impacting upon their costs and revenues. However, irrespective of the type and number of divisional structures comprising a particular firm, central management will still take all of the major decisions relating to the overall future and direction of the firm, e.g. possible mergers and acquisitions.

Solution to Task 50:

Memorandum

To: Harry O'Neill

From: James Crown

Re: The advantages and disadvantages of divisionalisation

Harry,

Following our recent discussion, this memorandum outlines some of the primary advantages and limitations of divisionalisation.

Advantages

1. Taking advantage of local knowledge

Divisional managers are much more likely to possess local knowledge which central management may not have. As a result, this should better inform their decision making and may ultimately lead to enhanced decisions on their behalf.

2. Speed of reaction

If local managers can make their own decisions rather than having to request central management to do so, then the decision-making process is likely to be quicker. This can be critical if a business opportunity presents itself and requires a quick decision.

3. Offers enhanced training opportunities
The fact that local managers are making decisions themselves rather than simply implementing the decisions of central management should mean that these local managers are acquiring critical decision-making abilities which should benefit the entire firm in the long-run.

4. Behavioural benefits
Similarly, by taking their own decisions it should encourage local managers to perform to the best of their ability, as the results from their decision making is likely to impact directly on their performance evaluation and promotional prospects, etc… From the opposite perspective, local managers who are simply implementing central management's decisions may not be overly motivated.

5. Easier organisational expansion/contraction
By breaking up a firm into a number of divisions, it should allow the overall firm to either add (expand) or delete (contract) a division as required. With a centralised structure, this may not be as easily achievable.

Limitations
1. Duplication of work
With divisionalisation it is likely that some divisions' maybe duplicating work performed in another division(s) as each may not be aware what the other is doing. For example, the same customer information may be stored on a number of divisions' computer systems simultaneously which results in additional unnecessary cost for the firm as a whole.

2. Flow of information
It is difficult to decide on the amount of information that should flow between each division and headquarters. If there is too little information flowing between the two, then a division may make decisions that are not in the overall firm's best interests. Conversely, if there is too much

information flowing between both parties, it resembles a centralised structure and defeats the purpose of divisionalisation.

3. Dysfunctional behaviour

When decision making power is vested with divisional management, there is a possibility that they may take decisions which may not be in the overall firm's best interests. Similarly, divisional management may begin to compete excessively with other divisions in an attempt to outperform them in the eyes of central management.

4. Lack of functional expertise

Many recently formed divisions may not necessarily have the functional expertise necessary to compete in their chosen markets. For example, the marketing department may have previously been located centrally, but when divisions are formed, the necessary expertise may not exist at the local level.

Solution to Task 51:

Report

To: Harry O'Neill

From: James Crown

Re: A comparison of the alternative divisional performance measures

Harry,

This report reviews the following divisional performance measures, all of which are currently used by ABC Ltd;

1. Profit
2. Return on Capital Employed (ROCE)
3. Residual Income (RI)
4. Economic Value Added (EVA)

1. Profit

Profit (sales revenue less expenses) is one of the most widely used performance measures due to the fact that many stakeholders rely on this measure to determine how firms' with whom they have an interest have performed in their most recent trading period. From a divisional perspective, the use of profit is particularly appropriate for divisions who operate as profit centres.

However, there are a number of disadvantages to using profit as a means of evaluating divisional performance. Most of these relate to how the profit figure itself is calculated (e.g. before/after interest/tax). Also, depending on the particular accounting rules and regulations adopted, different divisions may report different profit levels for the same set of transactions. Therefore, care is needed in determining and comparing profit figures across divisions, particularly in different jurisdictions.

While profit maybe suitable as a means of comparing divisional performance, it has been suggested that when evaluating managerial performance, controllable contribution may represent a better approach, as it measures the ability of managers to effectively use the resources under their control. Controllable contribution is calculated by deducting from total divisional revenues all those costs that are controllable by the divisional manager.

2. & 3. Return on capital employed (ROCE) & Residual income (RI)

I will compare these performance measures together, as they share many of the same strengths and weaknesses. In the terms of their calculation, the following applies;

ROCE = (net profit/capital employed) × 100%

RI = (net profit − interest on capital employed)

As both of these measures incorporate "net profit", then the issues outlined in (1) above are also relevant here.

Strengths

1. Both measures are simple to calculate and understand. However, RI may be slightly less "accessible" due to the inclusion of a notional interest charge as per the formula above.

2. They are both based upon profit and capital data which is readily available from any firm's accounting records. Therefore, there is little or no cost involved in their calculation.

Limitations
1. Absolute v comparative
ROCE as a % does not reflect the size of the divisional investment, nor does it indicate how much "better off" or "worse off" the overall firm is as a result of a particular division's performance. RI as an absolute measure does address the latter issue, but does not resolve the former. ROCE as a % provides a better basis for comparison, but ultimately neither measure is superior.

2. Target return/cost of capital
It may be very difficult to determine an appropriate cost of capital for particular divisions, especially if they are located in different countries. Nevertheless, the fact that different economic sectors may be subject to different degrees of risk, would suggest that a different cost of capital may be applicable to each. This being the case, comparisons in performance should be made by comparing the extent to which a division has succeeded in attaining their own particular target. If a firm applies the same target to all divisions, it may be too high in relation to low-risk divisions, thereby tempting them to pursue high-risk strategies to the possible detriment of the overall firm.

3. Accounting policies
There are a number of different but equally acceptable methods to calculate items such as depreciation and stock values. If different divisions are using different methods then their results may need to be standardised before valid comparisons can be made. Similarly, different divisions will have assets of varying ages, so to ensure a valid comparison the firm may need to restate each divisions' assets at their; (1) full acquisition cost, (2) current replacement cost, or (3) disposal value.

4. Divisional v managerial performance
It's incorrect to assume that a poorer-than-expected ROCE or RI is automatically a reflection of poor management. If this scenario does occur,

then it should prompt further investigation rather than becoming a "witch-hunt". Many aspects of good management may never be apparent from ROCE / RI such as; good employee relations or satisfied customers. As a result, firms (divisions) are increasingly relying upon both financial and non-financial measures when determining divisional and managerial performance.

Whilst the calculation of ROCE and RI often yields the same outcome, when differences do occur, the use of RI is always preferred, as it is regarded as a more robust performance measure.

4. Economic value added (EVA)

EVA extends the RI measure by attempting to approximate a firm's (division's) economic profit. EVA recognises that all capital has a cost, and earning more than the cost of capital should be the objective for firms (divisions).

The major difference between RI and EVA is that the latter measure includes adjustments to a division's financial performance measure (i.e. profit) for distortions introduced by accounting rules (e.g. GAAP). The formula for EVA is as follows;

EVA = (conventional divisional profit ± accounting adjustments − cost of capital charge on divisional assets)

Note: (conventional divisional profit ± accounting adjustments = economic profit)

Strengths

The accounting adjustments included in EVA allow divisions to avoid the immediate write-off of value-building expenditures, e.g. research and development, marketing, etc.. By doing so, it results in the capitalisation of these items, and spreads these costs over the period in which the benefits are expected to be received, i.e. the medium to long-term. Consequently, managers will not bear the full costs of the discretionary expenditures in the period in which it was incurred, and are therefore less inclined to take short-term decisions (e.g. asset acquisition and disposal decisions).

By making increases in economic profit a priority, the EVA of a division (or firm) should increase, which should then increase their market value and ultimately their share price. As a result EVA is regarded by some as the best indicator of firm (divisional) performance.

Limitations

Potential disadvantages of EVA include deciding on an appropriate cost of capital to be used (similar to RI). Furthermore, the decision in terms of the accounting adjustments to be included would appear to be very subjective and owing to their potential complexity, consulting firms are often used to determine which adjustments are relevant. Such consultants are often expensive and time-consuming, so a cost-benefit analysis is therefore needed to determine their viability.

Solution to Task 52:

Calculations

To: Harry O'Neill

From: James Crown

Re: Calculations pertaining to divisional performance

Harry,

Based on the information provided, I have calculated the following performance measures for each of ABC Ltd's three divisions;

1. Profit
2. Return on Capital Employed (ROCE)
3. Residual Income (RI)
4. Economic Value Added (EVA)

1. Profit

	France	Germany	Spain
Sales	1,560,000	1,750,000	2,500,000
Less costs			
Direct materials	300,000	400,000	500,000
Direct labour	150,000	165,000	180,000
Production overheads	85,000	100,000	130,000
Depreciation	50,000	42,000	60,000
Rent & Rates	35,000	40,000	43,000
Administration	65,000	73,000	80,000
R&D	200,000	300,000	500,000
Website	55,000	40,000	90,000
Marketing	80,000	65,000	100,000
Advertising	50,000	60,000	90,000
General expenses	25,000	20,000	15,000
Utilities	10,000	8,000	7,000
Training costs	50,000	75,000	100,000
Bad debts	20,000	15,000	12,000
Insurance	8,000	10,000	11,000
Patent costs	25,000	30,000	40,000
Total costs	**1,208,000**	**1,443,000**	**1,958,000**
Net profit	**€/£352,000**	**€/£307,000**	**€/£542,000**

2. Return On Capital Employed (ROCE)

ROCE = (net profit/capital employed) × 100%

France: (€/£352,000/€/£4,000,000) × 100%= **8.8%**

Germany: (€/£307,000/€/£5,000,000) × 100%= **6.14%**

Spain: (€/£542,000/€/£9,000,000) × 100%= **6.02%**

3. Residual Income (RI)

RI = (net profit − interest on capital employed)

France: €/£352,000 − (€/£4,000,000 × 7%) = **€/£72,000**

Germany: €/£307,000 − (€/£5,000,000 × 7%) = **(€/£43,000)**

Spain: €/£542,000 − (€/£9,000,000 × 7%) = **(€/£88,000)**

4. Economic Value Added (EVA)

EVA = (conventional divisional profit ± *accounting adjustments* − cost of capital charge on divisional assets)

To calculate EVA, we need to firstly determine each division's economic profit (conventional divisional profit ± *accounting adjustments*)

	France	Germany	Spain
Net profit	352,000	307,000	542,000
Add back			
R&D	200,000	300,000	500,000
Website	55,000	40,000	90,000
Marketing	80,000	65,000	100,000
Advertising	50,000	60,000	90,000
Training	50,000	75,000	100,000
Patents	25,000	30,000	40,000
Costs to be capitalised	**460,000**	**570,000**	**920,000**
Economic profit	**€/£812,000**	**€/£877,000**	**€/£1,462,000**

Please Note: I'm assuming that each of the six costs listed above can be wholly regarded as value creating activities, hence why they're included in my calculation of economic profit. I am further assuming that the benefit from these expenditures will be realised over the period of a single year, otherwise these costs would be spread over the number of years in which the firm expects to receive a future benefit from these newly capitalised assets. However, I fully appreciate that these are very subjective assessments which maybe open to challenge.

186 STRATEGIC FINANCE AND MANAGEMENT ACCOUNTING TOOLKIT

EVA can now be calculated as follows;

France: €/£812,000 – (4,000,000 × 7%)   =   **€/£532,000**

Germany: €/£877,000 – (5,000,000 × 7%)   =   **€/£527,000**

Spain: €/£1,462,000 – (9,000,000 × 7%) =   **€/£832,000**

Summary:

	France	Germany	Spain
Net Profit	€/£352,000	€/£307,000	€/£542,000
ROCE	8.80%	6.14%	6.02%
RI	€/£72,000	(€/£43,000)	(€/£88,000)
EVA	€/£532,000	€/£527,000	€/£832,000

Analysis:

As each division operates in a different country with different inflation rates and general economic circumstances, I cannot make direct comparisons between them. However, based on my calculations, I can make the following observations;

1. France

France made a net profit of €/£352,000 last year. It exceeded the 7% target rate by generating a ROCE of 8.8%, which in turn meant that its RI was positive at €/£72,000. When economic profit was taken into account, its EVA was €/£532,000, demonstrating that this division created real wealth for ABC Ltd's shareholders last year. As this division operates as a profit centre, then the profit measure is the most appropriate measure of divisional performance here.

2. Germany

Despite making a profit of €/£307,000 last year, Germany did not reach the 7% target rate of return as their ROCE was only 6.14%. This invariably meant that their RI was negative at (€/£43,000). However, this division did invest heavily in value creating assets during the year resulting in an EVA of €/£527,000. As this division was established as an investment centre, then RI and EVA would be the most suitable measures of divisional performance.

3. Spain

Spain made the highest profit of €/£542,000, but with a ROCE of 6.02% meant that they did not reach the firm's cost of capital threshold of 7%. Consequently, their RI was negative at (€/£88,000). However, this division invested heavily in value creating activities throughout the year and as a result their EVA was positive at €/£832,000. As this division also operates as an investment centre, then RI or EVA would be the most appropriate measures by which to evaluate their past performance.

Finally, I think it's important to stress that while certain performance measures are more suitable for certain divisional forms (e.g. the profit measure for a profit centre), a combination of measures should always be used to evaluate divisional performance as each measure tells us something different about the recent trading performance of a particular division.

Solution to Task 53:

Memorandum

To: Harry O'Neill

From: James Crown

Re: The possible dysfunctional consequences of short-term measures of performance

Harry,

Following our recent telephone conversation, this memorandum outlines some of the possible dysfunctional consequences of using short term measures of performance such as profit, ROCE and RI.

The main issue here is that if managers are evaluated on the basis of short-term measures of performance, they will focus their attention on maximising these measures and may therefore make decisions that are not necessarily in the firm's long-term interests.

For example, a manager may not invest in a particular project as the costs involved will result in reduced profits and hence ROCE and RI will fall in the short-term. However, this project may be beneficial to the firm in the long-run, but as the manager knows that s/he will be evaluated on the basis of short term measures of performance, they may not be willing to wait for the long-term benefits to accrue in case it jeopardises their short-term promotional and bonus prospects.

This is not an easy issue for firms, as on the one hand, stakeholders are looking for firms to increase their profits each year, but on the other hand, value creating activities often cost a lot of money while the benefits may not be realised for many years. In an attempt to overcome the dysfunctional consequences of using short-term measures of performance, firms can:

1. Lengthen the performance measurement period beyond a one year time horizon, as the longer the measurement period, the more congruent accounting measures of performance are with economic income. The disadvantage of this suggestion is that if rewards are provided a long time after the original actions were taken, there is a danger that they will lose much of their motivational impact.

2. Supplement the financial measures of performance with some non-financial items (e.g. Balanced Scorecard) that measure those factors critical to the long-term success of the firm, e.g. quality, innovation, productivity, etc.

3. Adopt the use of Economic Value Added (EVA) as it includes accounting adjustments which reflect the long-term costs involved in investing in value-creating activities.

PERFORMANCE MEASUREMENT 189

Solution to Task 54:

<u>Report</u>

To: Harry O'Neill

From: James Crown

Re: The potential ethical dilemmas which can occur in the management of divisional performance

Harry,

As you requested, the following are some of the potential ethical dilemmas which can occur in the management of divisional performance;

1. A major ethical dilemma with the management of divisional performance relates to the situation whereby divisional managers take decisions in their own self-interests, and not in the best interests of the overall firm. Firms can attempt to overcome this possibility by lengthening the performance measurement period, introducing non-financial measures of performance and adopting EVA.

2. If central management (i.e. head office) realise that a particular division is not operating as they would like (e.g. not taking advantage of potential opportunities), then at what point, if any, do they step in and take control. If true divisionalisation is to occur, then central management should let the division learn by their mistakes even if it means that the overall firm will not perform to their full potential in the short-term. By taking control, central management is effectively ending the policy of divisionalisation which may result in a loss of motivation and confidence on the part of divisional management.

3. From a central management perspective, it may be difficult to treat all divisions equally and fairly all of the time. Even if senior management favour one division over another, they should aim to ensure that they are objective in all of the evaluations that they perform.

4. When reporting their financial performance to head office, divisional management may attempt to make their performance look better than it actually was (e.g. understating liabilities, fictitious sales, understated costs, etc.). Central management should make it known that they will not tolerate this, but if it occurs they should take action immediately.

5. If a divisional manager feels that one of his / her colleagues in another division is performing better than s/he is, they may decide to try and undermine the performance of the other division in an effort to regain parity in terms of bonuses and promotional prospects. For example, if a transfer pricing opportunity presents itself which is of benefit to both divisions, s/he may ensure that a price cannot be agreed and therefore no transfer can occur.

Solution to Task 55:

Report

To: Harry O'Neill

From: James Crown

Re: An explanation of the fundamentals of transfer pricing

Harry,

As you requested, this report will examine the following areas;

1. An explanation of the context of transfer pricing
2. The aims of transfer pricing
3. The approaches available in transfer pricing
4. Possible conflicts in transfer pricing

1. An explanation of the context of transfer pricing
Transfer pricing is the price charged when one segment of a firm (e.g. a division) sells goods (or services) to another segment of the same firm (e.g. a different division). Like any commercial transaction, the selling division would like the price to be as high as possible, whereas the buying division wish to pay the least amount possible.

It's important to note that any transfer pricing transaction has no effect on a firm's overall profitability, as all that happens is that money is transferred from one division to another and no wealth is created for the overall firm. However, transfer pricing can have a big impact on a division's profitability (and hence managerial performance appraisal) depending on the transfer price set.

2. The aims of transfer pricing

The primary aims of transfer pricing are as follows;

1. To provide information that motivates divisional management to make good economic decisions, i.e. should they engage in transfer pricing or should they continue to buy/sell their produce from/to the external market. By making the "correct" decision, divisional management can improve their own division's profitability as well as the overall firm's profitability.
2. To provide useful information for evaluating the managerial and economic performance of divisions based on the fact that transfer pricing can have a big impact on a division's profitability.
3. To intentionally move profits between divisions/locations. This is especially true where a company has a number of divisions operating in a number of different countries, each of which may have a different corporation taxation rate. By selling goods/services from one division to another, a firm may be able to limit their overall corporation tax liability.
4. To ensure that divisional autonomy is not undermined. By allowing divisional management to decide whether or not to engage in transfer pricing, the spirit of divisionalisation is upheld.

3. The approaches available in transfer pricing

The following approaches are commonly used when setting transfer prices;

1. Set the transfer price at the external market price
2. Set the transfer price at the variable (marginal) cost price
3. Set the transfer price at the full cost price
4. Set the transfer price at cost-plus a mark-up
5. Allow the buying and selling managers to negotiate their own transfer price

4. Possible conflicts in transfer pricing

Unfortunately, no single transfer price is likely to be able to satisfy all four aims simultaneously and consequently management are often forced to make trade-offs. Specifically, owing to their very nature the decision-making and

192 STRATEGIC FINANCE AND MANAGEMENT ACCOUNTING TOOLKIT

performance evaluation aims are likely to conflict. For instance, the manager of a particular division may choose not to sell goods to another division at a certain price if they can sell the same goods externally at a higher price, even though this may not be in the overall firm's best interests. Also, deciding on an acceptable transfer price is likely to cause conflict on occasions between the buying and selling divisions.

Solution to Task 56:

Memorandum

To: Harry O'Neill

From: James Crown

Re: The alternative approaches available in setting transfer prices

Harry,

This memorandum outlines the various approaches to price setting available to Murphy Ltd should they decide to engage in transfer pricing with Smith Ltd;

1. The cost based methods
    1a. Marginal cost transfer prices
    1b. Full cost transfer prices
    1c. Cost plus transfer prices
2. The market method
3. The negotiated method

1a. Marginal cost transfer prices

When the external market for the good (service) to be transferred is imperfect, or even non-existent, marginal cost transfer prices can motivate the buying and selling divisions to operate at output levels that will maximise overall firm profits, but only in the short-run. Marginal costs may not be constant over the entire range of output because step increases in fixed costs can occur, and as a result measuring marginal cost is difficult beyond a short time period. Economic theory suggests that in the absence of a capacity constraint, the use of a marginal cost transfer price is the theoretically correct transfer price to encourage total firm optimality. Where a capacity constraint does exist, it has been suggested that goods (or services) should be transferred at the marginal cost plus the opportunity cost incurred as a result of the capacity constraint.

However, this form of transfer price has been criticised for providing poor information for evaluating the performance of both divisions as, the selling division will record a loss due to the fact that none of their fixed costs are included in the sales price, while the receiving division's profits may be overstated for the same reason. Consequently, there is low usage of this form of transfer pricing in reality.

1b. Full cost transfer prices

This form of transfer pricing is widely used in practice as managers generally view product-related decisions as long-run. Here, the selling division can recover their full-costs of production, although the fact that no profit will be obtained may understate their profits and act as a disincentive to supply internally.

A common criticism of this approach is that from the selling divisions perspective there is no incentive to control costs, as they are simply passed onto the next division. Similarly, costs derived from traditional costing systems can provide poor estimates of long-run marginal costs, so, ideally, full cost transfer prices should be derived from an Activity Based Costing (ABC) system.

1c. Cost plus transfer prices

This approach enables the selling division to obtain a profit margin on goods/services transferred and can be achieved by using either:

1. Full costs plus a mark-up
2. Variable costs plus a mark-up (this mark-up is intended to cover both the fixed costs and a profit contribution)

The use of this approach will cause inter-divisional transfers to be less than the optimal level for the firm as a whole, and if there are more than two divisions involved, the % margin becomes huge when a mark-up is added by the final division in the process.

2. Market based transfer prices

This approach is relevant when there is an external market for the transferred product or service. If the selling division has no idle capacity, then the market price is the perfect choice for the transfer price. Where the selling costs for internal transfers of the good or service are identical to those that arise from sales in the external market, the firm is indifferent as to where the good/service is sold.

Where idle capacity exists the situation is more difficult. If the selling division cannot make a profit in the long-run at the current market price, the overall firm would be better off either not to produce the product internally or to obtain its supply from the external market. If the buying division cannot make a profit in the long-run with transfers at the current market price, the firm would be better off either stopping production of the product or allowing the selling division to sell all of its output to the external market.

The selling division will incur selling expenses for external sales, whereas these costs may not be incurred for internal sales. Therefore, in reality many firms modify the market price when pricing inter-divisional transfers and deduct a margin to take account of the savings in selling expenses.

Some of the limitations of market-based prices are that there is no incentive for the buying division to purchase internally, although this may not be the best option from the firm's perspective. Also, the market price may be a temporary one induced by adverse economic conditions or dumping. Finally, many products do not have an equivalent market price, so the price of a similar, but not identical, product might be chosen. In this situation, the option to buy/sell on the open market does not really exist.

3. Negotiated transfer prices

In this approach the transfer price is agreed upon between the buying and selling divisions. Its use is most appropriate where some external market imperfections exist for the product / service involved, such as different selling costs for internal/external sales or where several different market prices exist. For any proposed transfer price – there is an upper limit (determined by buying division) and a lower limit (determined by selling division). The actual transfer price can fall anywhere between these two limits which is called the range of acceptable transfer prices.

There are two main advantages associated with negotiated transfer prices as follows:

1. It preserves the autonomy of the divisions as it allows the managers themselves to agree on a price.
2. The managers of the individual divisions are likely to have much better information about the potential costs and benefits involved in the transfer than others (i.e. central management) in the firm.

Negotiated transfer prices are inappropriate where there is a perfect market for the good/service, as in such a scenario there is no need for the managers involved to engage in negotiation. On the other hand, where there is no external market, it is unlikely that the managers can engage in meaningful negotiation.

The following limitations apply to negotiated transfer prices:-

1. As the final transfer price can depend on the negotiating skills and bargaining power of the individual managers involved, the final outcome may not be optimal.
2. They can lead to conflict between divisions which may require central management intervention to resolve.
3. Measurement of divisional profitability can be dependent on the negotiating skills of the individual managers, who may have unequal bargaining power.
4. They are time-consuming for managers especially when there are a large number of transactions involved.

Solution to Task 57:

<u>Report</u>

To: Harry O'Neill

From: James Crown

Re: Potential sources of conflict in transfer pricing and resolution strategies

Harry,

As demonstrated by the various approaches available in setting transfer prices, there are numerous conflicts that can arise between the buying and selling divisions which, depending on their severity, may result in a failure to agree on an acceptable transfer price. In an effort to overcome such difficulties, there are two options available to firms, both of which I will now outline.

1. Adopt a dual-rate transfer pricing system

A dual rate transfer pricing system uses two separate transfer prices to price each inter-divisional transaction. For example, the selling division may receive a full cost plus a mark-up on each transaction which is designed to approximate the market price of the goods / services transferred, while the buying division may be charged at the marginal cost of conducting the transfer. The difference in costs is resolved by a simple accounting calculation.

This method is not widely used in practice for a number of reasons;

1. It causes confusion when transfers spread beyond two divisions
2. It is considered to be artificial
3. It reduces divisional incentives to compete effectively
4. It is possible for all divisions to report profits when the firm as a whole is loss making

2. Transfer at a marginal cost plus a fixed lump-sum fee

This approach is applicable where the external market for the good/service is imperfect or non-existent, and the selling division has no capacity constraints. In this approach, all transfers are priced at the short-run marginal cost. The buying division is also charged a fixed fee for the privilege of obtaining these transfers at short-run marginal cost, and this fee is designed to cover a share of the fixed costs of the selling division and also provide a return on capital.

As a result of using this approach, both divisions should be able to report profits from inter-divisional trading. A further advantage of this approach is that it stimulates planning, communication and co-ordination between the divisions as both must agree on the capacity requirements so as to determine the bases for the fixed fee.